POSTMARKS
OF THE
AUSTRALIAN FORCES
FROM ALL FRONTS
1939 To 1953

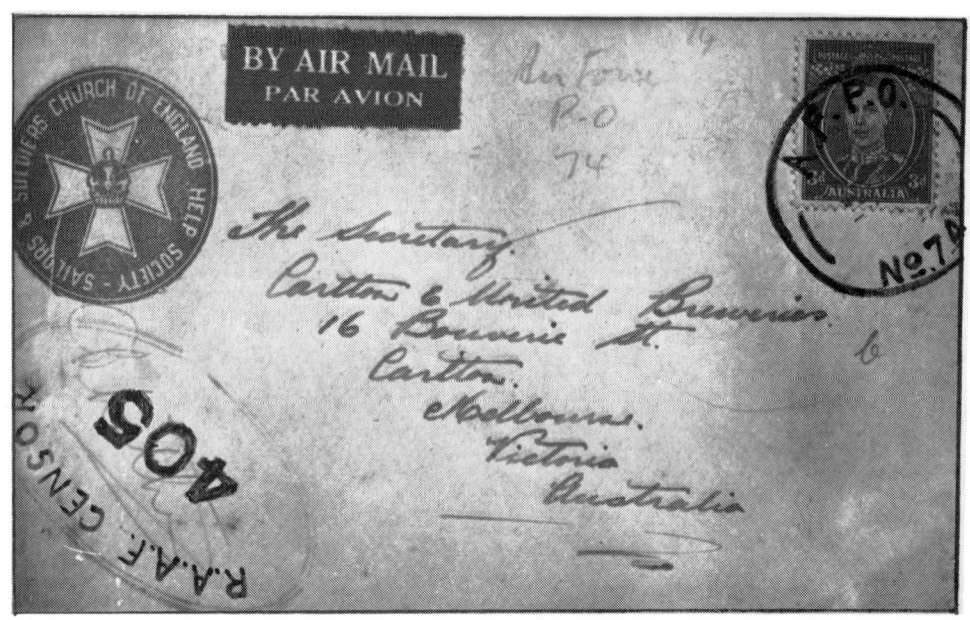

A.F.P.O. No. 74 – Port Moresby, Papua

"Tombstone" Censor Mark: "From H.M. Ships Passed by Censor" Signature and date

POSTMARKS

OF THE

AUSTRALIAN FORCES

FROM ALL FRONTS

1939 To 1953

By STEPHENSON STOBBS

Published by
Harry Hayes,
48-50 Trafalgar Street,
Batley,
West Yorkshire, WF17 7HA.

Originally published as a Supplement to the
Bulletin of the Australian Commonwealth Specialists'
Society of Great Britain, in twelve monthly parts,
commencing on September, 1954.

Second edition, extensively revised by the author,
published in 1976 as Harry Hayes Philatelic
Study No. 21.   ISBN 0 905222 13 X

Reprinted in 1984 by Harry Hayes.   ISBN 0 905222 49 O

Printed and made in Great Britain by
The Northway Printing Co. Ltd.,
51 Bingley Road,
Saltaire,
Bradford BD18 4SB.

POSTMARKS OF
THE AUSTRALIAN FORCES
From all Fronts, 1939 to 1953

Compiled by
STEPHENSON STOBBS

Foreword to the Original Edition, 1954

It is now over ten years since I started amassing my collection of Forces covers and from then right up to the present time I have steadily and consistently added thereto. From the very beginning, however, it became apparent that it was going to be extremely difficult to ascertain how many different marks were used; by whom they were used, etc.

Little or no information was forthcoming from official sources. During the time the war was being fought this was quite understandable, but since it is now some considerable time since hostilities ceased it is felt that the 'veil' might now be lifted — provided, of course, an official record was kept as to whom each particular mark was allocated, (which is very much doubted!!).

The writer has, over the years, kept a careful record of all the information which has come his way and in this connection he is particularly indebted to two philatelic pals 'Down Under', namely, Jack Leek and Tom Scott, and to certain members of the Australian Commonwealth Specialists' Society of Great Britain, namely, I. Ash, H.G. Lacey, H.S. Hughes, H.V. Sixsmith, and last but by no means least, D.D. Storms, who have duly reported to him every new mark which they acquired or encountered; and to all of whom he tenders his most grateful thanks.

Even with all this help, it is still realised that there is much information which is required before even a rough 'picture' can be obtained. If, however, a start — be it lacking in very many details — is not made then the object will never be attained, and it is said "that fools rush in where angels fear to tread" so this "fool" has, after much 'prodding', endeavoured to compile a CHECK LIST of all the marks which are known to him or which have been reported to him from one source or another. Whilst there have appeared in the philatelic press articles on certain marks used by the Australian Forces in the various Campaigns, it is thought that no complete listing has ever been attempted — probably because all sensible students of this branch of philately realised that it was nearly an impossible task! Among the chief articles to which attention may be drawn are —

"Australian Imperial Forces in Malaya; Postal History"
    by Harry S. Porter, F.R.P.S.L.
"Forces Postmarks of Malaya"
    by Harry S. Porter, F.R.P.S.L.
"Forces Postmarks of Malaya"
    by E. Jagger
"Postal History of 2nd. A.I.F."
    by Harry S. Porter, F.R.P.S.L.
"Australian Imperial Forces in New Guinea"
    by Evan Gill.
"British Army Field Post Offices 1939-47"
    by Col. G.R. Crouch and Norman Hill.
"Middle East Postal & Censor Markings 1939-45"
    by Major T.L.C. Tomkins.
"Middle East Censor Markings on British Field Post Office Covers 1940-45"
    by J.A. Firebrace.

"Markings on Australian Naval Mail"
    by Norman Hill.
"Forces Post Offices and Postmarks in Egypt 1939-47"
    by E. Jagger
"Forces Postmarks — Darwin Area"
    by J.E. Leek.
"Royal Australian Navy — World War II"
    by Harry S. Porter, F.R.P.S.L.
"Royal Australian Air Force Postal Service"
    by Harry S. Porter, F.R.P.S.L.

In spite of such a large list it will be noted that there has been very little written or listed concerning the Pacific Campaigns.

The CHECK LIST has been compiled by listing all the same type of postmark together (i.e. those with same wording) and by arranging each section in numerical order. Where possible the location where the mark was used is given as well as the Campaign but it will be realised that some of the marks were used from many different places as the particular Unit or Brigade using the mark moved around. In those cases the more important places only are given. With regard to the dates, there may be very many earlier and, for that matter, later ones to be recorded but, as stated previously, this list must only be regarded as a start.

In the "Remarks" column where the Unit or Brigade which used the particular mark is known this is shown as well as other small points which may be of interest.

The various types of mark will now be mentioned separately —

AUS FPO (See illustration No. 5)

These postmarks were made up of loose type borrowed from the Palestinian Government. Hence, in some postmarks, the number appears at the top whereas in others it is at the foot and in '35' and '37' the number is found at first at the top, whereas later on it was changed to the bottom.

It is doubtful whether '26', '28' and '38' were ever used by the Australian Troops and if anyone has definite evidence one way or the other it would be greatly appreciated.

It should be mentioned also that, in the Check List, in order to save space the movements of certain of these marks have been telescoped and the different 'journeyings' backwards and forwards as between Palestine, Libya, Syria, Egypt and back to Palestine again have not been shown in full detail.

AUST F.P.O. (Illust. No. 1)

All the postmarks of this type were only used in the Pacific Campaign. According to official records these were issued on 29th November, 1942, but it is extremely difficult to know what to do for the best as it is felt that a large number of these marks did not come into actual use until a much later date. It was therefore decided not to show this particular date for all the marks until some further evidence is forthcoming that they were, in fact, in use in 1942.

FIELD P.O. (Illust. No. 7)

Again all these marks were used in the Pacific Campaign and it will be noted that a nought appears before each number.

FIELD POST OFFICE (Illust. No. 6)

The exact remarks as set out above for "FIELD P.O." apply also for this mark.

FIELD POST OFFICE (Double Large Circle)

This is really a Malayan cancellation which was used by all Troops during the Malayan Campaign.

A.I.F. FIELD P.O. (Illust. No. 11)

Many of these marks were used in the North African Campaign, Palestine, or Syria before being returned to Australia to be issued to Troops employed in the Pacific Campaign. It is therefore essential to exercise great care in the reading of the "dates" before allocating these to any particular place (or Campaign).

AUST FIELD P.O. (Illust. No. 19)

All these marks were used in the Malayan Campaign, chiefly in the closing stages (namely 1945).

A.I.F. ARMY P.O. (Illust. No. 12)

It is believed that these five marks were used by Troops stationed in Australia.

AUST ARMY P.O. (Illust. 3 & 4)

Here again all this type of mark were employed in the Pacific Campaign and later some of the numbers went with the Australian Occupation Troops to Japan and later still to Korea.

It should be noted that only the first two numbers of this type, namely 0130 and 0131, have the figure '0' before them.

ARMY POST OFFICE (Illust. 9)

This type of mark — all of which have a nought preceding the number — was used in the Papua or New Guinea Sections or alternatively in the supporting areas of Northern Australia.

ARMY P.O. (Illust. 10)

The early numbers having a combination of letters and figures were taken by the Australian Troops to Palestine or Egypt and then returned with these Troops when they came back to take part in the Pacific Campaign.

The other numbers, varying from 0102 to 0135 — note figure '0' in front — were all used at places on the Australian Continent.

AUST UNIT POSTAL STN (Illust. 8)

As the name implies, these marks — and there are a large number of them — were used by Units which were scattered over a very wide field in connection with the Pacific Campaign — ranging from North West Borneo to New Ireland and even Nauru. Some of the marks are very scarce and much further information is required in this section.

UNIT POSTAL STATION (Illust. 13, 14, 15, 16, 17 & 44)

The remarks concerning "AUST UNIT POSTAL STN" apply even more so to the "UNIT POSTAL STATION" cancellations, except that the marks were usually applied by Units stationed on the Australian Continent. Very often such a mark was used by a small body of men maintaining a section of a Line of Communication — hence the reason why there are so many different marks and why they are not too easy to come across.

These marks are usually found to have been applied in bright blue, purple or red, and may be circular, oval or rectangular or square — varying considerably in design. One design, for example, is a double rectangle which has also incorporated in the mark a swan and a boomerang!

While it has been possible to allocate the majority of the letters which precede many of the numbers it is still not known to what the following letters were given —

VA.
X.
Y.
and Z.

BASE P.O. (Illust. 22 & 24)
AUST BASE P.O. (Illust. 21)
AUST ADV BASE P.O. (Illust. 23)

These three marks, as the words imply, were applied on mail emanating from the various Australian Bases, but the marks, which are quite common, are also to be found as 'back-stamps' on much of the mail, particularly on Registered letters. Naturally these marks come from the Bases on all the battle-fronts on which the Australian Troops served.

BGE. H.Q.P.O. (Illust. 18)
BDE. H.Q.P.O.

These marks were used by the Australian Troops when they went to Egypt and Palestine in 1940, but did not appear to have gone into use again after the Australian Forces returned to their own country for the Pacific Campaign.

It should be noted that the FIRST Brigade only used the letters 'BGE' in their postmark, while the SECOND AND THIRD Brigades used 'BDE'.

DIV H.Q.P.O. (Illust. 25)
DIV. SUPPLY H.Q.P.O. (Illust. 20)
RAILHEAD P.O. (Illust. 40)

Three further marks which were used by the Australian Troops chiefly during their sojourn in Palestine. Again it would not seem that any of these marks were used on the return of the Troops to the Australian Area.

A.F.P.O. (Illusts. 30, 31 & 35)

All these marks were used by Air Force Units during the Pacific Campaign. Care should be taken to note that some of the postmarks have 'No.' before the figures while the same number can also be found without this 'prefix' — usually the two different types have been used at two separate places. The numbers '28' and 'No. 30' have the addition of 'R.A.A.F. JAPAN' in the marks.

AIR FORCE P.O. (Illusts. 32 & 43)
AIR FORCE POST OFFICE (Illust. 34)

The same remarks set out above for the "A.F.P.O.' postmarks apply to these two marks also. "No. 71" has the addition of "QLD. AUST" in the mark.

"R.A.A.F. AUSTRALIA" (Illust. 27)

There are many different marks of this type each with a four-figure number. Those with a four thousand number come from New South Wales; those with a five from Victoria; with a six from Queensland; with a seven from South Australia; with an eight from Western Australia; and with a nine thousand figure — only one, "9600" — from Tasmania.

R.A.A.F. P.O. UNIT
R.A.A.F. BASE P.O. (Illusts. 26, 33, 37, 41 & 45)

All these marks, with the exception of the two additional types of "R.A.A.F. BASE P.O. No. 4", consist of a single circle with two bars across — one slightly above and the other slightly below the diameter. By far the majority of the marks are found on re-directed R.A.A.F. letters (used as back-stamps).

With regard to the two additional types of R.A.A.F. BASE P.O. No. 4" — which, incidentally, I have only ever seen used on re-directed mail — these are—

a) In the ordinary double circle English style, or
b) In the same type as the English Slogan Postmark.

The latter has two slogans which, from the covers in my collection, were used alternatively, namely—

A.F.	IF UNDELIVERED	R.A.A.F.	ADVISE R.A.A.F.	RA
P.O.No4	IN SEVEN DAYS	BASE P.O. No.4	BASE P.O. PROMPTLY	BAS
— P.M.	RETURN TO R.A.A.F.	5 — P.M.	OF EACH CHANGE	5 —
II 44	BASE POST OFFICE	29 MCH 44	OF ADDRESS	29

It would therefore appear that this was a 'machine', as opposed to a 'hand' cancellation.

R.A.N. POST OFFICE

As Naval Bases were set up in the Pacific so these Circular postmarks came into use. It seems that the marks were applied to mail sent by personnel from these Bases and not from the ships calling there — the mail from which was postmarked by one or other of the 'dumb' cancellations (i.e. no indication of the whereabouts of the particular boat being given in the mark.)

NAVY POST OFFICE

Only one circular mark of this type is known and this carries in addition to the above words "No. 1". This mark was used by Navy personnel at Darwin.

NAVY P.O.

There are two marks, both straight line ones, bearing these words; one having the addition of "No. 1" and the other "DARWIN N.T." — both were used from the Naval Base at Darwin.

H.M. TRANSPORT

Some marks have a number in addition to the above words, others just the words "H.M. TRANSPORT" alone — they speak for themselves. They are to be found both in a straight line (with several sizes of letters) and in normal circular form.

MILITARY POST OFFICES (Illust. 2)

There are many marks to be found bearing the words — "MIL. P.O." before the place name — all were used from Military camps in Australia.

W.A.A.A.F. POST OFFICES

I have only come across three of these marks, all from Women's camps in Victoria.

MILITARY HOSPITALS (Illust. 42)
REPATRIATION HOSPITALS (Illust. 38)

These speak for themselves, but, it should be mentioned that some Hospitals are still open and are still using their particular postmark.

R.A.A.F. POST OFFICES (Illusts. 28 & 36)

As in the case of "MIL. P.O." marks there are many different marks from "R.A.A.F. P.Os." situated at or in Air Force camps or Air Fields in Australia.

NAVAL POST OFFICES

These marks were used by Naval personnel from their different camps or barracks in Australia.

R.A.N. SHORE ESTABLISHMENTS

I have never seen any of these marks, which I am assured do exist, so that if anyone can assist in this connection it will be greatly appreciated.

ENGLISH CANCELLATIONS

An endeavour has been made to list the postmarks used by the British Forces which are to be found on Australian stamps or which are known to have been used by the Australian Forces: it is quite realised that this is a "tall order" as the use of some marks may have been purely fortuitous – as when an "Aussie" visited a British camp and posted a letter while there or alternatively gave a British "Tommy" a letter to post for him.

However, certain Australian Troops were attached to British Units and consequently many of these marks were quite genuinely used.

EGYPTIAN CANCELLATIONS

Many of these marks bearing the words "EGYPT POSTAGE PREPAID" (followed by a number) are to be found cancelling Australian stamps or are known to have been used by certain Australian Troops – hence the same remarks apply as in the previous English marks.

INDIAN CANCELLATIONS
NEW ZEALAND CANCELLATIONS

The remarks for the English and Egyptian cancellations again apply.

AMERICAN CANCELLATIONS

Although I have worked for some years on a list of these marks I now understand that one of our members, who is far more competent than me to deal with such a subject, is already working on such a list, which, when ready, will be made available to members. I have consequently decided to omit this section.

Anyone who can add any information, no matter how small, is invited to communicate with the compiler who will greatly appreciate any additions, amendments, criticisms, or alterations to this check list.

Note to the Second edition, 1976:
Thanks are extended to Bob Emery for his help in providing the covers for illustration.

A.I.F. P.O. No. 201 — Milne Bay, Papua

Aust F.P.O. 162 — Wharf Area, New Britain

INDEX TO POSTMARKS

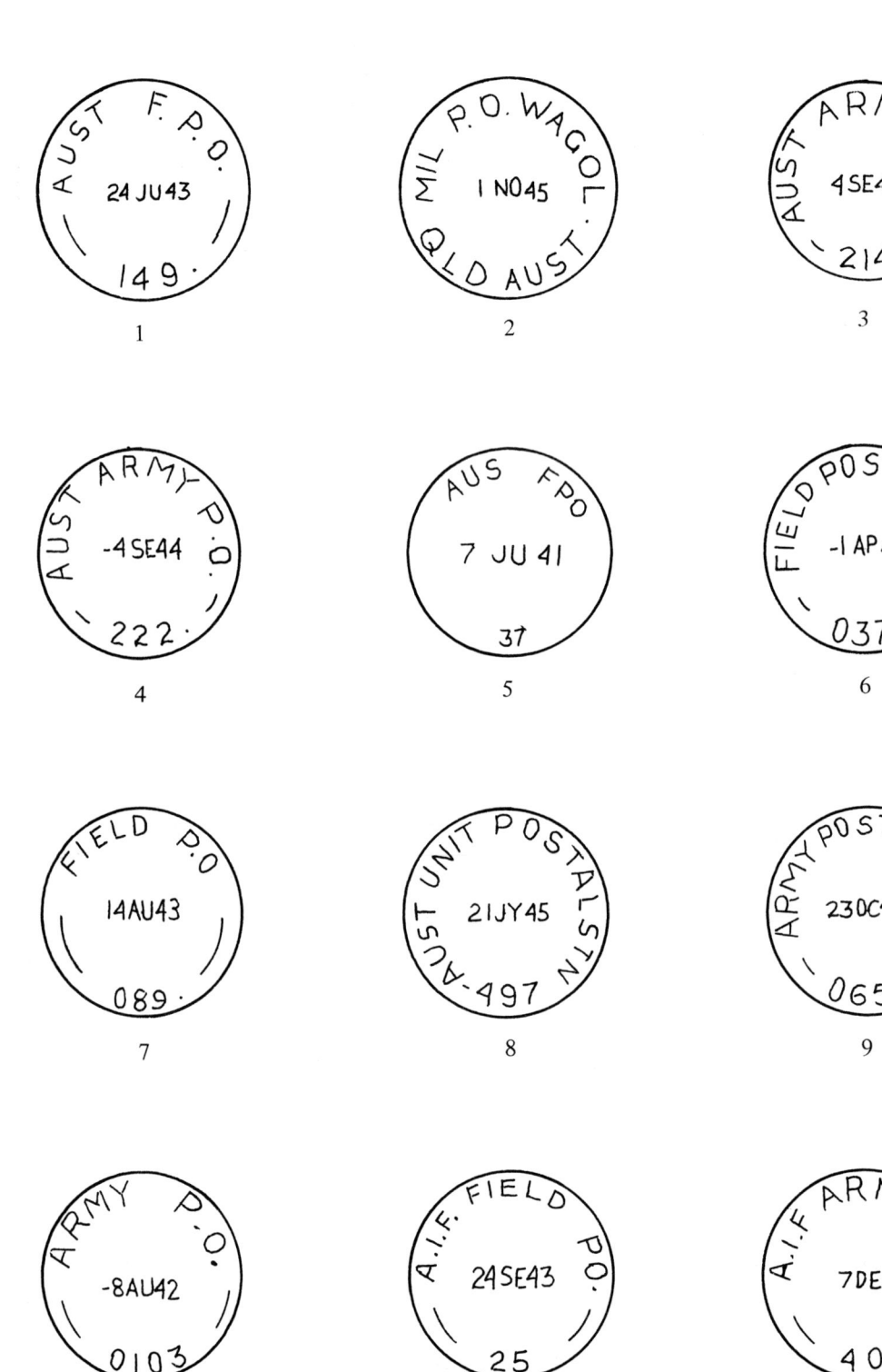

AUST F.P.O.
24 JU 43
149

1

MIL P.O. WAGOL
1 NO 45
QLD AUST

2

AUST ARMY P.O.
4 SE 44
214

3

AUST ARMY P.O.
-4 SE 44
222

4

AUS FPO
7 JU 41
37

5

FIELD POST OFFICE
-1 AP 43
037

6

FIELD P.O
14 AU 43
089

7

AUST UNIT POSTAL STN
21 JY 45
-497

8

ARMY POST OFFICE
23 OC 42
065

9

ARMY P.O.
-8 AU 42
0103

10

A.I.F. FIELD P.O.
24 SE 43
25

11

A.I.F ARMY P.O.
7 DE 41
40

12

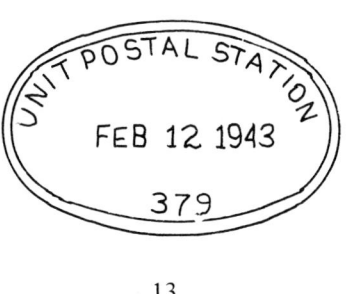

UNIT POSTAL STATION
FEB 12 1943
379

13

UNIT POSTAL STATION
17 AUG 1943
WII

14

UNIT POSTAL
-7 JUN 1945
STATION E.L.C. 12

15

UNIT POSTAL STATION
S.84
13 JUL 1943

16

UNIT POSTAL
7 NOV 1943
Station Y17

17

1ST BGE HQ. P.O.
14 SE 40
M 1

18

AUST FIELD P.O.
251

19

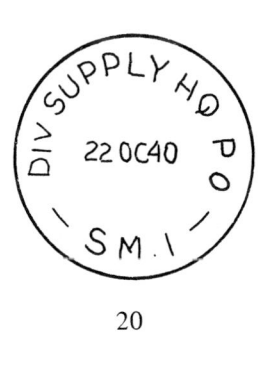

DIV SUPPLY HQ PO
22 OC 40
S.M. I

20

N°7 AUST BASE P.O.
1200 HRS · 20 JA 41
I

21

BASE P.O
27 JA 42
B.W.I

22

N°7 AUST ADV BASE P.O.
1500 HRS 6 AU 44
A

23

BASE P.O. 7 MD
28 OC 41
017

24

15

DIV HQ. P.O.
30 OC40
D.M. 1

25

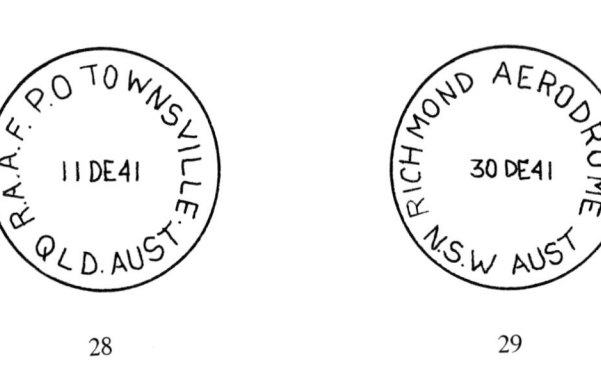

Nº11 R.A.A.F BASE P.O.
23JE45
PACIFIC

26

R.A.A.F. 6300
13AP44
AUSTRALIA

27

R.A.A.F. P.O TOWNSVILLE
11DE41
QLD. AUST

28

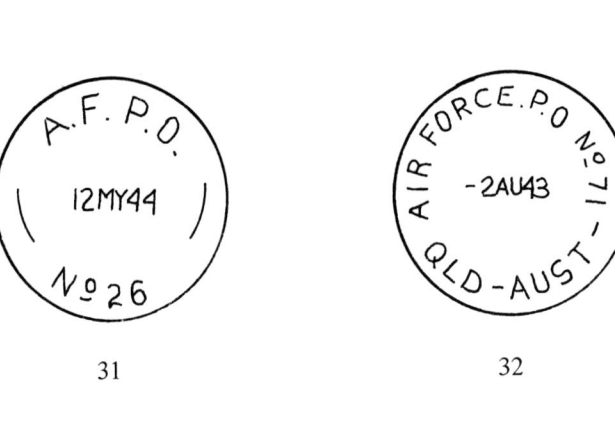

RICHMOND AERODROME
30DE41
N.S.W AUST

29

A.F.P.O. Nº30
16DE48
R.A.A.F. JAPAN

30

A.F. P.O.
12MY44
Nº 26

31

AIR FORCE.P.O Nº71
-2AU43
QLD-AUST

32

R.A.A.F.
BASE PO Nº4.
9FE42
ENGLAND

33

AIR FORCE. POST OFFICE
7 MY45
Nº 252

34

A.F.P.O.
MAY 3 1942
No. 14

35

R A A F
POST OFFICE
17 JAN 1944
Nº S215

36

37

38

39

40

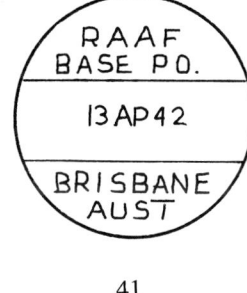

41

42

43

44

IF UNDELIVERED
IN SEVEN DAYS
RETURN TO R.A.A.F.
BASE POST OFFICE

R.A.A.F.
BASE P.O. No4
5 — PM
29MCH44

ADVISE R.A.A.F
BASE PO PROMPTLY
OF EACH CHANGE
OF ADDRESS

45

Field Post Office 020 – Papua

A.I.F. Field P.O. No. 21 – Milne Bay, Papua

18

Postmark	No.	Place	Campaign	Earliest Date	Latest Date	Remarks
AUS FPO	26	Nazeiret	Palestine)	It is doubtful		
	28		do.)	whether these two		
				marks were ever		
				used by Aus: Troops		
	31)	Ikingi Maryut	do.	16. 3.41	1. 4.41	No. @ Top
	31)	Tobruk	North Africa	12. 4.41	18. 8.41	18th BDE
	31)		Palestine	15.11.41	18.12.41	No. @ Top
	32)		Palestine	9. 3.41	12. 5.42	(7 DIV.H.Q.
	32)		Syria	−. 6.41		(No. @ Foot
	33	Tobruk	North Africa	6. 5.41	20.10.41	No. @ Foot
	33)		Syria	16.11.42	−. 7.42	(20 BDE
	33)		Palestine		−.10.42	(No. @ Foot
	34	Tobruk	North Africa	23. 4.41	23.10.42	No. @ Top
	35)	do.	do.	26. 6.41	2. 9.41)	1 DIV.
	35)		Syria	27. 5.42	24. 9.42)	First appeared @ Top, later @ Foot − 24 BDE.
	36	Tobruk	North Africa	2. 4.41	12. 8.41	No. @ Top.
	36		Syria	27. 5.42	25.10.42	(26 BDE − 9 DIV.
	37	Tobruk	North Africa	7. 3.41	17.12.41)	(No. @ Top. No. first
	37		Syria	−. 6.42	)	appeared @ Top, later @ Foot.
	38			It is doubtful if		
				this mark was ever		
				used by Aus. Troops		
AUST. F.P.O.	146	New Guinea	Pacific	29.11.42	10.11.43	2 Armd. Div.
	147		do.	29.11.42	10. 5.43	2 Armd. Div.
	148		do.	29.11.42	20. 5.43	2 Aust. Armd. Div.
	149		do.	29.11.42	27.11.43	do. do.
	150		do.	29.11.42	22. 9.44	1 Div. N.S.W.
	151		do.	29.11.42	24. 7.43	do.
	152		do.	29.11.42	10. 7.43	28 BDE.
	153		do.	28. 9.43	18.11.43	
	154		do.	10. 7.43	6. 8.44	
	155	Strawberry W.A.	do.	22.12.42		
	155	New Guinea	do.	22. 2.43	25. 7.43	2 DIV. 5 BDE.
	156	New Guinea	do.	12.12.42	−. 5.45	8 BDE.
	157	Papua Milne Bay	do.	28.10.42	6. 3.44	
	157	New Britain	do.	3. 3.45	22.11.45	4 BDE. 5 DIV.
	158	New Guinea	do.	29.11.42	17. 6.45	3 DIV.
	159	Bougainville	do.	23. 7.43	1. 6.45	3 Aust. DIV.
	160	Bougainville	do.	23. 2.44	4.12.45	
	161	Wau	do.	19.12.42	13. 9.45	
	162	Wharf Area, N.B.	do.	29.11.42	20. 9.44	4 DIV.

LOOSE TYPE POSTMARKS BORROWED FROM PALESTINE GOVT.

ARMY

Postmark	No.	Place	Campaign	Earliest Date	Latest Date	Remarks
	163	Darwin	Pacific	1.10.43	16.12.45	2 BDE. 4 DIV.
	164	Port Moresby	do.	14. 8.43	23. 4.45	6 BDE.
AUST. F.P.O.	165	Western Australia	do.	13.12.44		13 BDE.
	166	Papua	do.	−. 1.43	9. 8.45	5 DIV.
	167	Rabual	do.	10. 1.43	12. 8.45	11 BDE.
	168	Papua	do.	7. 8.43	18. 6.45	11 DIV.
	169		do.	1. 1.43	15.12.43	
	170	Papua	do.	8. 3.40	1. 6.45	2 AUST. Corps.
	171	Papua	do.	28. 1.43	22. 4.44	5 DIV.
	172		do.	21.12.43		6 AUST. DIV.
	173		do.	29.11.42		6 AUST. DIV.
	174	Papua	do.	31. 8.43	10.10.45	7 DIV.
	175		do.	29.11.42	14.11.43	1st ARMY
	176		do.	29.11.42	2. 8.44	2nd ARMY
	177		do.	29.11.42	2. 8.44	do.
	178		do.	27.11.42		
	179		do.	27.11.42		
	180	Rabual	do.	13. 2.43	7. 1.46	
	181	New Guinea	do.	15. 4.43	28. 7.43	
	182	do.	do.	18. 5.43	14. 1.44	
	183		do.	28. 8.45		1st ARMY
	184	Bougainville	do.		3.12.45	1st ARMY
	185	Torokina Bougainville	do.	26. 6.45		(Rear H.O. 23 (Aust. Inf. BDE
	186	Northam	do.	16. 2.44	27. 4.44	3 CORPS
	187		do.			
	188		do.			
	189	Darwin, N.T.	do.	14. 6.43	1. 9.44	12 DIV.
	190	do.	do.	31. 7.44	1. 9.44	12 DIV.
	191	Eastbourne	G. Britain	28. 3.45	26. 5.45	
	192		Pacific	26. 8.43	18. 4.45	
	193	Bougainville	do.	−. −.45		
	194		do.			
FIELD P.O.	073	Australia	Pacific	31. 8.42	28. 5.45	2 CORPS
	074		do.	27. 2.43	29. 7.44	2 Armd. Div.
	075		do.	22.12.42		1 DIV.
	076		do.	29.11.42		2 DIV.
	077		do.	12. −.42	28. 2.45	11 DIV.
	078	New Guinea	do.	21. 8.42	5. 4.45	11 DIV.
	079	Milne Bay	do.	3. 8.42	27. 2.46	
	080)	Papua	do.	28. 1.42	7.12.42	
	080)	Tokyo (Hiro)	Japan	31. 5.47	10. 7.47	
	081	Dobodura, Papua.	Pacific	13. 8.43	23.11.45	

ARMY

Postmark	No.	Place	Campaign	Earliest Date	Latest Date	Remarks
FIELD P.O.	082	Oro Bay, Papua	Pacific	22. 3.43	7.12.45	
	083	Geelong, Aust.	do.			3 Armd. Div.
	084	Torokina	do.	27. 6.42	26. 2.45	3 DIV.
	085		do.	11. 8.44	3. 9.44	4 DIV.
	086		do.	17. 4.43	21. 4.45	
	087		do.			
	088		do.	14. 9.44	29. 9.44	
	089	Darwin, N.T.	do.	19. 6.41	16. 8.45	12 BDE. 12 DIV.
	090	Lae, N.G.	do.			12 BDE. 12 DIV.
	091		do.	27. 5.42		
	092		do.	5.10.45		
	093		do.			
	094	Thursday Island	do.	26. 3.43	9. 4.46	5 DIV.
	095	New Guinea	do.	7.10.42	11. 1.43	3 Armd. Tank Bde.
	096		do.	4. 5.43	8. 3.45	1 ARMY
	097		do.	17. 8.42	27. 3.44	1 ARMY
	098	New Guinea	do.	6.11.44	29. 8.45	1 ARMY
	099)	Queensland	do.	1. 1.43	30. 8.43)	1 ARMY also in Purple, dia.
	099)	Dobodura	do.	26. 4.44	)	40 m.m.
	099)	Lae, N.G.	do.	28. 9.45	)	1 ARMY
	0100	Warwick	do.			
	0101	Thursday Island	do.	2.10.42	25. 9.43	
	0102)	Darwin, N.T.	do.	17. 4.42	12. 9.44	23 BDE.
	0102)	Bougainville	do.	28. 2.45	22. 7.45	do.
	0102)	Rabual	do.			do.
	0103	Cairns, Qld.	do.	12. 7.42	28. 5.44	
	0133	Queensland	do.			
	0136)	Darwin, N.T.	do.	6. 9.42	22. 4.43	13 BDE.
	0136)	New Guinea	do.	28. 8.44	28. 4.43	
	0137	Darwin, N.T.	do.	12. 4.42	22. 5.43	12th DIV.
	0138	Papua	do.	14. 4.41	9. 2.45	
	0139	Milne Bay	do.	30. 5.42	2.10.45	
	0140	Port Moresby	do.	19.10.42	13. 6.45	
	0141	Papua	do.	25. 9.42	21.12.44	N.G. FORCE
	0142	Papua	do.	11. 2.43	1. 3.43	
	0143		do.	30. 7.43		
	0144		do.			
	0145		do.			
FIELD POST OFFICE	019	Port Moresby	Pacific	1. 2.43	1. 9.43	
	019	Saroa, New Guinea	do.	12. 3.45	1.11.47	

ARMY

Postmark	No.	Place	Campaign	Earliest Date	Latest Date	Remarks
FIELD POST OFFICE	020	Papua	Pacific	29. 1.42	22. 7.45	ISLANDS
	021	Townsville	do.	12. 3.42	12. 7.42	
	022	New Guinea	do.	30. 3.42	24. 6.42	
	023		do.	1. 7.42	16. 9.44	
	024	Rear Details N.Z.	do.			HQ 17 Aust. Inf. BDE
	025	Queensland	do.	8. 7.42	5.11.42	P/Mark retired 1942
	026	Atherton, Qld.	do.	22.12.42		
	026	Borneo	do.	4. 4.44	8. 9.45	1 CORPS
	027	Morotai, N.E.I.	do.		2. 2.46	
	028	Morotai, N.E.I.	do.		−. 1.46	
	029		do.	13. 5.42	2. 6.42	1 AUST. Armd. Div.
	030		do.	25. 4.42	17. 2.43	
	031	New South Wales	do.	9. 3.42	−. −.43	1 DIV.
	032	Australia	do.	9. 3.42	13. 8.42	
	033	Morotai, N.E.I.	do.	9. 4.45	2. 2.46	9 Aust. Div.
	034		do.	−. −.42	12. 2.46	do.
	035		do.	30. 7.43	25. 9.45	do.
	036	New Guinea	do.	17. 5.42	28. 2.45	do.
	037	Taraken	do.	1. 4.42	30. 9.45	
	038	Papua	do.	17. 1.44	10. 3.45	
	038	Sarawak	do.	30. 4.45	2. 2.46	
	039	New South Wales	do.	7. 6.42	18. 4.44	2 ARMY
	040	do.	do.	2.12.42	2. 8.44	2 AUST. ARMY
	041	do.	do.	16. 9.42	28. 7.44	2 ARMY, 2 DIV.
	042	Port Moresby	do.	27.12.42	26. 2.45	
	043		do.	19.10.42	9. 3.43	3 Armd. Div.
	044		do.			do.
	045		do.			do.
	046	Melbourne	do.	6. 7.42	22. 3.43	do.
	047		do.	8. 6.42	11. 9.42	
	048	Queensland	do.	16. 5.42	11.11.42	
	049	Alice Springs	do.	7.10.43		
	050	Banka Banka	do.	3. 8.43		
	051		do.	27. 1.42	14. 9.42	
	052		do.	7. 3.42	18.11.42	11 Aust. Div. Postal Unit
	053		do.	27. 1.42		
	054		do.	24. 1.44		
	055		do.	22. 5.42	9.11.42	
	056		do.			
	057	Merridin	do.			
	060	Finschhafen	do.	6. 8.44		
	068	Milne Bay	do.	10. 8.41	21.10.44	7 BDE.11 Div.

ARMY

Postmark	No.	Place	Campaign	Earliest Date	Latest Date	Remarks
FIELD POST OFFICE	069	Bougainville	Pacific	1. 2.43	6. 9.45	29 BDE. 5Div.
	070		do.			
	072	N.T. Adelaide River	do.	20. 4.42	8.11.43	12 DIV.
	S.P.501	Singapore	Malaya	25. 9.40	17. 1.42	Double Circle
	S.P.502		do.	8.10.40	6. 6.41	do.
	S.P.503		do.	17.10.41		do.
	S.P.504	Kota Bharu	do.	10. 2.41	3. 1.42	do.
	S.P.506		do.			do.
A.I.F. FIELD P.O. No.	5	Egypt	North Africa	9. 7.41	−.10.42	A.P.O.5 (Aust. Convt. Depot)
	6	Mughazi	do.	3. 7.41	26.10.42	
	7)	do.	do.	9. 7.41	26. 1.42	
	7)	Port Moresby	Pacific	2. 3.44	13. 9.44	
	8)	Nazeiret	Palestine	9. 7.41	25.10.42	
	8)	Port Moresby	Pacific	−. 3.44	20. 5.45	
	9)	Rafah	Palestine	8. 2.41	21.10.41	
	9)	H.M. Transport	Pacific	31. 3.42	31. 5.42	
	10	Hill 69	Palestine	9. 7.41	25.11.42	
	11	Jerusalem	do.	15. 7.41	10.12.42	
	12)		North Africa	7.12.41	11.12.41	Corps Postal Unit
	12)	Milne Bay	Pacific	29.11.42	26. 9.44	1st Corps
	12)	Bougainville	do.	23. 2.45	26. 8.45	
	13)		Syria	14. 7.41	30.10.41	Corps Adv. H.Q.
	13)	New Guinea	Pacific	14.10.42	18.10.44)	1 Aust. Corps
	13)	Port Moresby	do.	23. 4.45	)	
	14)	Haifa	Palestine	19. 7.41	13.12.41	
	14)	New Guinea	Pacific	8. 7.42	22. 9.45	1 Aust. Corps
	15)		North Africa	15. 8.41	10. 5.42	
	15)	Bougainville	Pacific	31. 5.43	8. 8.45	1 Corps
	16)	Cairo	North Africa	16.10.41	19.11.41	
	16)	Lae, N.G.	Pacific	16. 9.44	25. 9.44	1 Corps
	17	Seremban	Malaya	6. 2.41	13. 1.42	
	18	Johore	do.	22. 2.41	5. 2.42	
	19	do.	do.	27. 8.41	15. 1.42	
	20		do.	26. 9.41	2.12.41	
	21)	Egypt	North Africa	4. 7.41	11.12.41	6 Div. Supply
	21)		Ceylon	−. 3.42	13. 7.42	
	21)		Pacific	20. 6.44	1. 9.45	6 Div.
	22)		North Africa	18.10.41	13.12.41	
	22)	Borneo	Pacific	20. 8.44	11. 5.45	
	23)		Syria	−. 7.41	−. 1.42	
	23)		Ceylon	22. 3.42	−. 7.42	16 BDE. 6Div.

ARMY

Postmark	No.	Place	Campaign	Earliest Date	Latest Date	Remarks
A.I.F. FIELD P.O. No.	23)	Papua	Pacific	6.10.43	13. 9.45	
	24)		Syria	5.10.41	15. 1.42	17 BDE. 6 DIV.
	24)		Celon	5. 2.42	−. 7.42	
	24)	New Guinea	Pacific	9.10.43	28. 8.45	11 DIV.
A.I.F. FIELD P.O.	25	Darwin, N.T.	Pacific	−. 3.42	22. 4.45	19th BDE.
	26	Nazeiret	Palestine	−. −.41		? ?
	27	Port Moresby	Pacific	9. 2.42	16. 3.45	21 BDE. 7 DIV.
	28)		North Africa	29.10.42	3. 3.45	
	28)		Japan	25. 3.45	12.10.45	7 DIV.
	29	Singleton, N.S.W.	Pacific	25. 3.41	10. 9.44	1 Armd. Div.
	30	New Guinea	do.	6. 3.42	21. 1.44	do.
	31		do.	15. 4.42	31.10.42	do.
	32	New Guinea	do.	22. 6.42	6.11.43	do.
	51		Pacific	30.10.42	28. 5.43	1 Armd. Div.
	52	Dobodura, Papua	do.	2. 4.42	14. 3.45	11 DIV.
	53	Papua	do.	18. 5.41	31. 1.46	7 DIV.
	54)		North Africa			? ?
	54)		Pacific	13. 7.42	16. 1.46	7 DIV.
AUST FIELD P.O.	246		Malaya			
	247		do.			
	248		do.			
	249	Bangkok	Siam	21. 9.45	30. 9.45	
	250	Changi	Malaya	15. 9.45	27.11.45	
	251)	P.O.W. Camp Singapore	Malaya	15. 2.42	5.10.43	
	251)	Changi	Malaya	15. 9.45	27.11.45	
A.I.F. ARMY P.O.	46		Pacific			
	47		do.	3.12.42	4. 6.43	
	48.		do.			
	49.	Alice Springs N.T.	do.	24. 9.42	25. 4.45	
	50	Banka Banka, N.T.	do.	31. 8.44	14. 3.45	
AUST ARMY P.O.	0130	Victoria Barracks, Melbourne	Pacific	25. 6.42	2. 7.46	
	0131		do.	15. 7.43		

ARMY

Postmark	No.	Place	Campaign	Earliest Date	Latest Date	Remarks
AUST ARMY						
P.O.	0131	Kure, Japan	Pacific	–. –.46	–. –.47	with B.C.O.F.
	196	Tolga Q	Pacific	19. 7.43	26. 9.44	
	196	Atherton Q	do.	29.12.44	7. 4.45	
	197	Thursday Island	do.	5.10.43	27. 5.48	Also in Purple – dia. 35 m.m.
	198	Queensland	do.			
	199	New South Wales	do.			
	200	do.	do.			
	201	Victoria	Pacific			
	202	do	do			
	203	Western Austr.	do.			
	204	Perth, W.A.	do.	23.10.44		
	205	Western Austr.	do.			
	206	Tasmania	do.			
	207	New Guinea	do.	16. 9.43	2. 2.46	
	208	Saidor	do.	4.11.43	26. 1.44	
	209	Madang	do.		31. 1.46	
	210	New Guinea	do.		2. 2.46	
	211	Finschhafen	do.	21. 5.44	22. 1.46	
	212	Madang	do.		1. 2.46	
	213	Milne Bay	do.	29. 6.43	23.12.44	7 B.P.O.
	214)	Lae, N.G.	do.	14. 1.44	19. 9.44	
	214)	Tokyo	Japan	17. 4.46	16. 4.49	
	214)		Korea	–. 6.50	30.11.52	
	215)	Port Moresby	Pacific	6.10.43	20. 9.45	
	215)	Kure	Japan	25. 4.48	7. 3.53	12 AUST L/C
	216)	Papua	Pacific	27. 7.43	1. 8.45	
	216)	Kyoto	Japan	29. 1.46	2. 4.51	
	216)		Korea	25.11.51	27. 8.53	
	217	Wewak	Pacific	29.10.43	29. 1.46	
	218	Milne Bay	do.	6. 8.43	8.11.43	Unit of 7 B.P.O.
	219	New Guinea	do.	4. 8.43		4 L. of C.
	220	do.	do.	25. 3. 43	8. 3.44	do
	221	Lae, N.G.	do.	16. 4.44	4. 6.45	do.
	222	Wau	do.	19. 5. 42	8. 6.44	4 L. of C. Postal Unit
	223	do.	do.	24. 6.44	17. 7.44	4 L. of C.
	224	New Guinea	do.			
	225	New Guinea	do.			
	226	Barry Springs	do.			
	227	Larrimah, N.T.	do.	11. 8.43	31. 1.44	
	228	Alice Springs N.T.	do.	23. 7.43	8.10.43	
	229	Larrimah, N.T.	do.	1. 4.44	21. 9.44	2 L. of C.
	230	Darwin, N.T.	do.	29.11.42	23. 3.46	A.P.O. (Also used on Naval mail)

ARMY

Postmark	No.	Place	Campaign	Earliest Date	Latest Date	Remarks
AUST ARMY P.O.	231	Batchelor, N.T.	Pacific	31. 8.43	27. 2.45	
	232	Darwin	do.	3. 3.43	30. 9.45	Used by Canadian Troops in Australia
	233	Katherine, N.T.	do.	3. 3.44	3. 4.45	
	234	Larrimah, N.T.	do.			
	235	do.	do.	9. 3.44		
	236	Adelaide River N.T.	do.	8. 5.43	15. 5.43	
	237	Alice Springs	do.	20. 3.44		
	238	Adelaide River N.T.	do.	3.11.41	28. 2.45	
	239)	Adelaide	do.	16. 3.45		
	239)	Borneo	do.	21. 7.45	26. 6.46	HQ. B.M.A., Borneo
	240	Morotai, N.E.I.	do.	23. 7.45	11.11.45	Gen. Details Depot.
	241	Eta Jima	Japan	31. 8.46	2.11.48	65 Inf. Battn.
	242	Merotai	Pacific	23. 7.45	2. 2.46	
	243	do.	do.			
	509	Tarakan	Pacific	29. 6.45	2. 2.46	6 DIV.
	510	Borneo	do.	8. 8.45	31. 1.46	
	511		do.		1. 2.46	
	512	Kaitachi	Japan	19. 6.49	13.12.49	
	513	Labuan	Pacific	—. —.45	31. 1.46	
	514		do.	20.11.45	1. 2.46	
	515		do.			
ARMY POST OFFICE	058	Port Moresby	Pacific	21. 3.42	1.11.44	
	059	Milne Bay	do.	30. 4.42	27. 9.44	
	060	Milne Bay	do.	3. 1.43	6. 9.45	
	061	Goondin Windi, Q.	do.	26. 5.42	27.10.46	
	062	Townsville, Q	do.			
	063	Rockville, Q.	do.			
	064	Maryborough	do.			
	065	Darwin, N.T.	do.	19. 2.42	18. 2.45	A.P.O. (Also on Naval mail)
	066	Pine Creek, N.T.	do.	13. 4.43	7. 3.45	
	067		Ceylon	—. 3.42	—.11.42	
	069		Pacific	8. 3.45		
ARMY P.O. A.M.1		Cairo	North Africa	15. 9.40	27. 9.41	

ARMY

Postmark	No.	Place	Campaign	Earliest Date	Latest Date	Remarks
ARMY P.O.	A.P.1	Jerusalem	Palestine	—. 2.41	12.12.41	L. of C. — A.P.O.11
	A.P.1	Geera, N.G.	Pacific	27. 1.42	15. 9.42	
	A.W.1)	Beit Jiria	Palestine	29.10.40	31. 7.41	A.P.O.4
	A.W.1)	Morotai	Pacific	6. 1.43	2. 1.46	
	No.1	Craigs Buildings Melbourne	Pacific	3. 9.40	4. 5.42	H.Q. A.I.F. Postal Unit
	0102		do.	13. 8.44		? Field P.O.
	0103	Cairns, Q.	do.	12. 7.42	8. 5.44	
	0104	Dubbo, N.S.W.	do.	15.10.42		
	0105	Tamworth, N.S.W.	do.	24. 6.42	20. 3.43	
	0106	Broadmeadow, N.S.W.	do.	1. 1.43	26. 5.43	
	0107	Victoria Barracks, Sydney	do.	10. 9.42	2. 8.43	
	0108	Liverpool, N.S.W.	do.	8. 7.42	23.10.42	
	0109	Bathurst, N.S.W.	do.	27.11.42		
	0110	Victoria Barracks Brisbane	do.	7.10.42	9. 8.43	
	0111	Port Moresby	do.	28. 5.43	30.10.45	Backstamp for all Islands mail (7 Base P.O.)
	0112	do. (Sogeri)	do.	16. 5.43	27.11.44	
	0113	Geelong, Vic.	do.	20. 7.42		
	0114	Mount Isa. Q.	do.	1.10.42	12. 8.45	
	0115	Camp Pell, Vic.	do.			
	0116	Seymour, Vic.	do.			
	0117	Noonamah, N.T.	do.	28. 8.42	2.10.44	11 DIV.
	0118	S. Australia	do.			
	0119	do.	do.			
	0120	Merridin W.A.	do.			
	0122	Western Australia	do.			
	0123		do.			
	0124		do.			
	0125	Launceston, Tas.	do.			
	0126	Mataranka, N.T.	do.	10. 2.43	21.10.44	
	0127	Adelaide River, N.T.	do.	29. 7.42	31.10.44	
	0128	Katherine N.T.	do.	10. 9.42	8. 5.44	

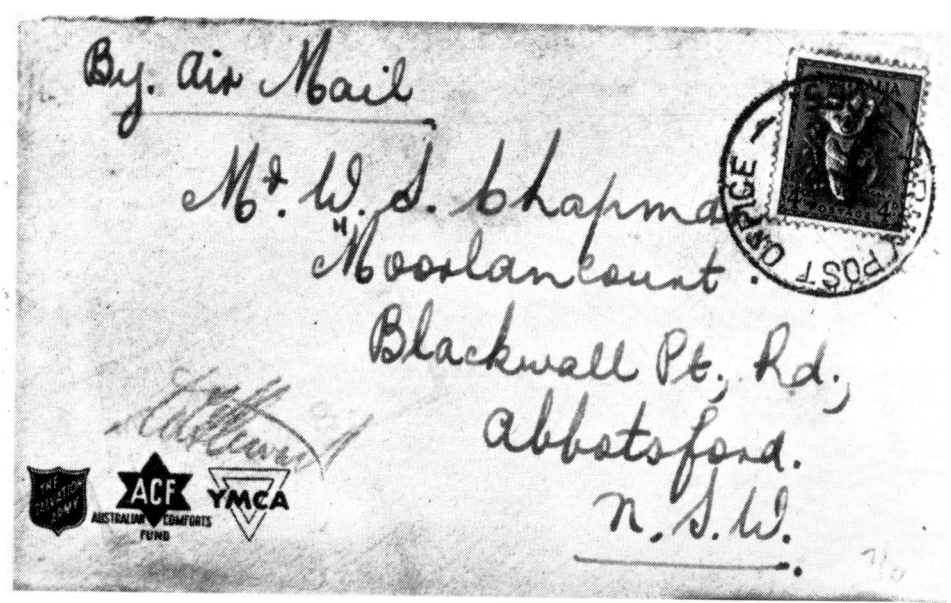

Army Post Office 065 – Darwin, N.T.

Aust Unit Postal Stn. 452 – Korea

ARMY

Postmark	No.	Place	Campaign	Earliest Date	Latest Date	Remarks
ARMY P.O.	0129	Larrimah N.T.	Pacific	4. 3.43	26. 2.45	
	0130	Melbourne, Victoria Barracks.	do.	24. 6.42	14. 8.43	
	0131	Melbourne	do.	13. 4.43	13. 8.43	
	0132	Milne Bay	do.	17. 5.42	27. 1.45	7 Aust. Base Postal Unit
	0133		do.			
	0134	Elliott, N.T.	do.	−. 8.43	16. 8.43	
	0135	Barrow Creek, N.T.	do.	21. 5.42	6. 3.45	
AUST. UNIT POSTAL STN.	302		Pacific			
	303	Mareeba	do.	12.12.43	25. 5.46	
	305	Torokina	do.	1. 3.45	18. 9.45	2/1 A.G.H.
	308		do.	6. 8.45	14.12.45	
	309		do.	8. 9.45	8.11.45	
	313	Nauru	do.	28.11.45	14.12.45	
	314		do.			
	315		do.			
	317		do.	21. 4.45	15. 5.45	
	318		do.	27. 6.43	31. 7.45	
	331		Pacific			
	333		do.	2. 4.44	27. 8.45	
	334	Merridin	do.	19. 1.44	18. 2.44	
	335		do.			
	336	Corunna Downs	do.	28. 8.44		CAMP 319
	337		do.			
	338		do.			
	339		do.			
	340		do.			
	341		do.			
	342	Nauru	do.	1. 3.44	20. 9.44	
	343		do.	6. 8.44	25. 9.44	
	344		do.	23. 9.44		
	345)	Darwin, N.T.	do.	15. 8.43	6. 9.45	2/1 Lt.A.A.
	345)		Japan			
	346	Northern Australia	Pacific	30.11.43	29.12.43	38 BN. 12 BDE.
	347	do.	do.	2. 2.44	23. 4.44	12 BDE.
	348	Darwin, N.T.	do.			13 BDE.
	349	Adelaide River, Darwin area	do.	2. −.43	24. 2.45	107 A.G.H.
	350	Northern Australia	do.	16. 8.43	3.11.44	12 BDE. 12 DIV.
	351	Darwin	do.	3.10.43	1. 8.44	12 DIV.

ARMY

Postmark	No.	Place	Campaign	Earliest Date	Latest Date	Remarks
AUST. UNIT POSTAL STN.	352	Darwin	Pacific	15. 8.43	–. 9.44	7 BN. 23 BDE.
	353	do.	do.	9.11.43		
	354	do.	do.	17. 9.43	8. 9.45	
	355	do.	do.	6.11.43		
	356	do.	do.			
	357	Katherine, N.T.	do.	1. 5.44		101 A.G.H.
	358	Darwin, N.T.	do.		–.11.43	28 Aust. Inf.
	359		do.	15.12.43		5 Aust. Inf.
	360	Ioma, Papua	do.	10. 8.43	31.12.45	5 Aust. L of C.
	361	2/9 A.G.H.	do.	17. 4.43	18. 9.45	N.G.F.
	362	128 A.G.H.	do.	20. 7.43	25. 9.44	N.G.F.
	363	WAU, New Guinea	do.	3. 5.43	6. 8.43	
	364	New Guinea	do.	23.12.43		
	365	WAU, N.G.	do.	10. 6.43	20. 9.45	HQ 47 Aust. Inf. Bde
	366	Shortland Island B.S.I.	do.	–.10.45	–.1. 46	
	367	Wau, N.G.	do.	15. 9.44		11 Aust Div., Postal Unit
	368	Bougainville	do.	21.11.44	14. 5.45	
	369	Bulola, Wau, N.G.	do.	–.12.43		
	370	do.	do.			
	371	Bera Bera, N.G.	do.			
	372		do.	3.10.43	15. 9.44	
	373	Treasury Islands, B.S.I.	do.	4.10.44	–. 4.45	
	374	Emirau, New Ireland	do.	6.10.44	15. 5.45	8 BN.23 BDE.
	375	Port Moresby	do.	28.10.43	13. 1.44	
	376		do.	20. 9.44	19. 2.45	Three types
	377		do.		31. 1.46	
	378		do.			
	379		do.	17.12.43	6. 2.44	
	386		Pacific			
	387		do.	4. 9.44		
	388)	Tokyo	Japan	12. 7.48		
	388)		Korea	–. 5.52	30. 7.54	2 BN.
	389		Pacific	15. 9.44		11 Aust. Div. Postal Unit
	390	Dobodura, Papua	do.	24. 1.44	6.10.46	
	391		do.	29. 7.44	30. 9.44	
	392	New Guinea	do.		2. 5.44	N.G. Force
	393		do.	4. 9.44	10. 5.49	7 Aust Base Postal Unit

ARMY

Postmark	No.	Place	Campaign	Earliest Date	Latest Date	Remarks
AUST. UNIT POSTAL STN	394		Pacific	1. 5.41		
	395	Milne Bay	do.	25. 4.45	10.12.45	
	396	New Guinea	do.		31.12.45	
	397	do.	do.			N.G.F.
	398	do.	do.			do.
	399	Militat	do.			do.
	400	New Guinea	do.			do.
	401	do.	do.			do.
	402	do.	do.	−. 4.44	15.11.44	
	403		do.	8. 8.44		
	405	Port Moresby	do.	28. 9.45	29.10.45	
	406		do.			
	407		do.		10. 9.44	4 Aust Div. Postal Unit
	408	Lae, N.G.	do.	5. 5.44		
	410	Lae, N.G.	do.	9. 1.44	24. 9.45	
	411		do.	21.12.44		
	412	Port Moresby	do.	10. 2.44	18. 3.45	
	413	Morgan Park Qld.	do.	15. 5.44		3 Aust L of C.
	414	Munna Point	do.	14. 4.44	21.11.45	do.
	415	Toorbul Point	do.	7. 7.44	11. 6.45	N.T. L of C.
	416	Timor (Port E.I.)	do.	11. 5.44	31. 3.46	
	417		do.			5 Aust. Inf.
	418		do.	29.12.43		
	419		do.	29. 5.44		2/8 Aust Command
	420		do.	13. 9.44		10/48 Aust Inf.
	421		do.			13 Detention Bks
	422	Larrimah, N.T.	do.			7 Aust. Army
	423		do.	17. 1.45	27. 2.45	108 Aust Con Depot
	424		do.			
	425		do.			
	426		do.			
	427		do.			
	428		do.			
	429		do.			
	430		do.			
	431		do.			
	432		do.	24. 9.44		
	433		do.	26. 7.44	20. 3.45	
	434	Lae	do.	25. 9.44	5. 3.45	
	435		do.			
	436	Cairns, Q.	do.	−. −.43	28. 1.45	
	437		do.			
	438		do.			
	439		do.	26. 7.45	29.11.45	

ARMY

Postmark	No.	Place	Campaign	Earliest Date	Latest Date	Remarks
AUST UNIT POSTAL STN	440	Moratai, N.E.I.	Pacific	10. 6.45	12. 2.46	2/5 A.G.H.
	441	East Borneo	do.	−. −.45		
	441	Labuan	do.	10.10.45		
	442	do.	do.			
	443	Labuan	do.			
	444	North-West Borneo	do. do.			
	445	Borneo	do.			
	446	Sarawak	do.			
	447	do.	do.			
	448	Jesselton, Borneo	do.	18.10.45		
	450		do.			
	452)		do.			
	452)	Kobe	Japan	30.11.45	24. 1.50	
	452)		Korea	−. 7.42	17.11.54	
	453)		Pacific			
	453)	Eta Jima	Japan	30.12.51		
	453)		Korea	7. 5.54	27. 7.54	130 Aust. Gen Hos.
	458		Japan	8. 5.57		
	495	Fukuyama	Japan	8. 5.47	26. 8.53	1st DAY 8.5.47) 65 Aust Inf
	496)	Mya Jima	do.	8. 9.46	14.12.51	116 Con. Depot
	496)		Korea	−. 6.52		
	497	Kure	Japan	6. 3.46	23.10.49	H.Q. Base
	498		do.			
	499		do.			
	500		do.			
	512	Katachi	do.			34 Inf Base
	513	Labuan	Pacific			
UNIT POSTAL STATION	29		Pacific			OVAL
	92		Pacific			do.
	106	Darwin	do.	22. 8.43	9.11.43	do. 10/48 BN.
	140		Pacific	13. 7.43		do.
	149		do.	17. 6.42	17. 1.43	do.
	369		Pacific			RECT.
	374		Pacific	−. 3.45		do.
	375		do.			do.
	376)		do.	23. 6.42		do.
	376)		do.	25. 5.42	3. 6.42	CIRCLE
	379		do.			RECT.

Postmark	No.	Place	Campaign	Earliest Date	Latest Date	Remarks
UNIT POSTAL STATION	1000		Pacific	29. 9.43		RECT.
	1008	Northern Territory	Pacific		−.11.43	RECT. A.G.H.
	1025	Darwin	Pacific			RECT.
	1047	Northern Territory	Pacific	4. 9.43		RECT. A.G.H.
	7 M.D.) Field) Postal) Unit)		Pacific			OVAL
	AC.36		Pacific			RECT.
	AC.37		do.	4. 7.44	2. 8.44	do.
	AC.39	Mundia, B.S.I.	do.	15.10.44	−. 3.45	do.
	AP.1		do.	23. 5.43	27. 6.43	RECT.
	AP.2	Victoria Barracks, Brisbane	do.	30. 9.42	6. 9.43	do.
	AP.3	Cooktown	do.	20.1. 43	9. 9.43	do.
	AP.4		do.	31.12.43		do.
	AP.5	Kleinton	do.	30. 8.43	20. 8.44	do.
	AP.6		do.			do.
	AP.7	Atherton	do.	11. 6.44	26. 7.44	OVAL
	AP.9		do.			RECT.
	C.A.	Alice Springs	do.			OVAL
	D.2.	Roper River N.T.	do.	9. 9.43	28. 9.44	OVAL
	D.5.	Brooks Creek, Darwin	do.		20. 9.44	do.
	D.6.	Darwin	do.			do.
	D.7.	do.	do.			do.
	D.9.	do.	do.	9.12.42	28. 9.44	do.
	D.10	do.	do.		18. 9.44	do.
	D.12	do.	do.	4. 5.42	23.12.42	RECT. A.G.H.
	D.13	do.	do.	15. 9.42	28. 9.44	do. A.G.H.
	D.14	do.	do.	31. 7.43	17. 8.43	OVAL
	D.17	do.	do.			do.
	D.19	do.	do.	11. 9.42		
	ELC 1	Kenmore, N.S.W.	do.	30.10.42	5. 3.44	RECT.
	ELC 2		do.			do.

Right-margin bracketed annotations:

- 2 AUST. CORPS (AC.36–AC.39): 112 AUST.) CON DEPOT)
- 1 AUST ARMY (AP.1–AP.9): (NORTHERN) COMMAND)
- DARWIN AREA (C.A.–D.19): 12 BDE. 13 AUST. DET. BRKS. / 12 DIV.
- ELC 1–ELC 2: 114 AUS GEN. HOSP.

ARMY

Postmark	No.	Place	Campaign	Earliest Date	Latest Date	Remarks	
UNIT POSTAL STATION	ELC 3	Australia	Pacific	30. 6.42	16. 6.44	RECT.	
	ELC 4		do.			do.	
	ELC 5		do.			do.	
	ELC 6		do.	2. 6.43		do.	
	ELC 7		do.	9. 8.44		do.	EASTERN LINE OF COMMUNICATION
	ELC 8		do.	28.12.43	6. 5.44	do.	
	ELC 9		do.	24. 4.43	3.10.44	do.	(Sometimes unframed)
	ELC 10		do.	24. 9.43		do.	
	ELC 11		do.	22.10.42	2. 6.44	do.	
	ELC 12		do.	4. 6.45	29.10.45	do.	
	ELC 13		do.	7. 8.45		do.	
	ELC 14		do.	24. 4.43		do.	
	ELC 16		do.			do.	
	ELC 17	Moruba, Q	do.	23.11.43	12.12.43	do.	
	ELC 18		do.	10.12.43	25. 6.45	do.	(Two sizes)
	ELC 19		do.			do.	
	ELC 20	Stoney Creek Q,	do.	3.12.43	15. 4.44	do.	2/2 A.G.H.
	ELC 21		do.			do.	
	ELC 22		do.			do.	
	ELC 23		do.			do.	
	ELC 24		do.			do.	
	ELC 25		do.			do.	
	ELC 30		do.			do.	
	E.21		Pacific			RECT.	
	E.22		do.			do.	
	E.23		do.			do.	
	E.25		do.			do.	
	E.26	Kingaroy, Q.	do.	5. 2.43	30. 6.43	do.	EASTERN COMMAND
	E.27		do.			do.	
	E.28		do.			do.	
	E.29		do.	6. 7.42	28.10.42	do.	
	E.30		do.	22. 9.42	11. 6.43	do.	
	E.97	N.S.W.	do.	28. 5.42		RECT.	1 AUST. DIV. UNIT
	E.98		do.			do.	
	E.101		do.			do.	
	E.102		do.			do.	
	E.103		do.			do.	
	E.104		do.			do.	EASTERN COMMAND
	E.105	Western Australia	do.		1. 5.44	do.	
	E.106		do.			do.	
	E.107		do.			do.	
	E.108	Western Australia	do.		30. 4.44	do.	
	E.109		do.			do.	
	E.110		do.	16. 7.42		do.	1 DIV.

ARMY

Postmark	No.	Place	Campaign	Earliest Date	Latest Date	Remarks	
UNIT POSTAL STATION	E.111		Pacific	28. 6.42	4.10.43	RECT.	
	E.113		do.			do.	
	N. 6		do.			OVAL	
	N. 8	Darwin, N.T.	do.	17. 6.42	28. 9.44	do.	12 DIV.
	N. 9		do.			do.	
	N.10		do.	14. 7.42	13. 8.43	do.	
	N.18		do.			OVAL	
	N.24		do.	5. 3.43	9. 3.43	OVAL	
	N.26		do.			do.	
	N.27		do.	6. 4.42	8. 4.43	do.	
	N.28		do.	4. 7.42		do.	
	N.28A		do.			do.	
	N.29		do.	29.11.42	1.12.42	do.	NORTHERN COMMAND
	N.30		do.	7. 7.42	1. 4.43	do.	
	N.31	Losuia, Papua	do.	4. 3.43		do.	
	N.32	Townsville, Q.	do.	24. 7.42		do.	
	N.32A		do.	20. 5.44	27. 3.45	do.	
	N.33		do.			do.	
	S.00		do.			RECT.	Probably should be S.100
	S. 4		do.			do.	
	S. 5		do.	6. 8.43		do.	
	S.10		do.			do.	
	S.14		do.	12.12.43		do.	
	S.15		do.			do.	
	S.17		do.	15. 6.43	20. 9.43	OVAL	
	S.18		do.			RECT.	
	S.20		do.			do.	
	S.25	Springvale	do.	5. 6.42		do.	
	S.30		do.		8. 9.43	do.	
	S.31		do.	23. 1.43	12. 4.43	do.	
	S.32		do.			do.	
	S.33		do.			RECT.	SOUTHERN COMMAND
	S.34		do.			do.	
	S.36		do.	12.4. 43		do.	22 Fld. Regt.
	S.38		do.			do.	
	S.40	Caboolture	do.		20. 9.43		1 Aust Army
	S.50		do.			RECT.	
	S.58		do.			do.	
	S.75		do.	25. 8.43	7. 9.44	RECT.	8 Aust. Cav. Reg.
	S.76		do.		28. 9.44	do.	
	S.77	Northern Australia	do.	5.10.43	20. 9.44	do.	2 BDE.

ARMY

Postmark	No.	Place	Campaign	Earliest Date	Latest Date	Remarks	
UNIT POSTAL							
STATION	S.78		Pacific	14. 4.43		OVAL	
	S.79	Darwin	do.	21. 7.42	12. 9.44	do.	8 BN.) 23 BDE.)
	S.80		do.			RECT.	
	S.81		do.	17.12.42	6. 8.43	OVAL	
	S.83		do.	22. 4.43		RECT.	
	S.84	Northern Australia	do.	11.11.42	28. 9.44	OVAL	12 BDE.
	S.85		do.			RECT.	
	S.86		do.	9.12.42	30. 3.43	do.	
	S.87		do.	9.10.42	20. 9.43	do.	
	S.89		do.		28. 9.44	do.	
	S.91		do.	7.11.42		do.	
	S.92		do.	20. 4.43	28. 4.43	do.	
	S.93		do.	4. 8.43	7. 8.43	do.	
	S.97		do.	23. 2.45		do.	
	S.99	Northern Australia	do.	13. 9.42	−.11.43	do.	13 BDE.
	S.101		do.	9. 2.43	2.11.43	do.	
	S.102		do.			do.	
	S.103		do.	23. 6.43		do.	
	S.104		do.			do.	
	S.105		do.			OVAL	
	S.183	Adelaide	do.	22. 5.42	22. 6.42	RECT.	
	S.193		do.			do.	
	S.194		do.	15. 6.44		do.	
	S.194		do.	13. 1.44	2. 8.44	OVAL	27 BN.
	S.195		do.	14. 6.42	20. 9.43	do.	
	S.197	Leave & Transit Depot, Marrickville, N.S.W.	do.	19. 5.44		RECT.	
	S.214		do.	22. 6.42	22. 9.44	do.	
	S.215		do.	29.11.43	7. 5.46	do.	(Large)
	S.216		do.			do.	
	S.221					do.	
	V.A.51		do.			do.	
	V.A.52		do.	20. 3.44	15. 4.44	do.	
	W.1		do.	20.12.42	20.12.43	CIRCLE	
	W.1		do.	29. 3.43		RECT.	(In Red)
	W.2		do.	12. 4.43		CIRCLE	
	W.3		do.			do.	
	W.4		do.			do.	
	W.6		do.	12.11.43	22.11.43	RECT.	
	W.7		do.			CIRCLE	
	W.10	York, W.A.	do.	27. 2.42		RECT.	

SOUTHERN COMMAND

ARMY

Postmark	No.	Place	Campaign	Earliest Date	Latest Date	Remarks
UNIT POSTAL STATION	W.11		Pacific	15.10.43	5. 6.44	do.
	W.12		do.	21. 6.43	7.10.43	do.
	W.13		do.	28. 9.43		OVAL (Small)
	W.13	Western Australia	do.	20. 8.42		CIRCLE
	W.14	Darwin, N.T.	do.	16. 7.42	23. 9.44	CIRCLE 13 BDE) 11 BN)
	W.15	Darwin, N.T.	do.	22.12.42	29. 8.44	do. 13 BDE) 16 BN)
	W.16	Darwin, N.T.	do.	1. 6.44	18. 9.44	do. 13 BDE) 28 BN)
	W.18		do.			RECT.
	W.19		do.	28. 9.43		do.
	W.20		do.			CIRCLE
	W.23		do.			do.
	W.24		do.			do.
	W.25		do.			do.
	W.26		do.			do.
	W.28		do.	26. 5.43		do.
	W.30	Swan Barracks, Perth.	do.	26. 8.43	28. 8.44	do.
	W.32		do.		20. 9.44	do.
	W.33		do.			do.
	W.34		do.			do.
	W.37		do.	25. 9.44		do.
	W.39		do.			do.
	W.41		do.	5.12.42		do.
	W.49		do.			CIRCLE
	L of C.X.1.		Pacific	17. 2.44	16. 3.44	OVAL 121 A.G.H.
	L of C.X.2	Adelaide River, N.T.	do.	16. 4.43		do.
	L of C.X.3	Larrimah, N.T.	do.	19. 6.43	16. 2.44	do.
	X1	Barrow Creek	do.	7. 10.43		
	X2	Bonella Bonka	do.		20. 9.43	
	X3	Elliott	do.	7.10.43		
	X4		do.	10.11.43		RECT.
	X.14		do.	15.11.43		do.
	Y.1		do.			Three Lines (Unframed)
	Y.4		do.			do.
	Y.5		do.	18. 7.43		do.
	Y.6		do.			do.
	Y.7		do.			do.
	Y.9		do.			do.
	Y.10		do.			do.
	Y.13		do.			do.
	Y.15		do.			do.

WESTERN COMMAND

7 Aust Army

2 Line of Comm., Darwin Area

ARMY

Postmark	No.	Place	Campaign	Earliest Date	Latest Date	Remarks
UNIT POSTAL STATION	Y.16		Pacific			Three Lines Unframed
	Y.17		do.	5.10.43	7.11.43	do.
	Z.1		do.			RECT. 2/7 Aust Div.
	Z.2		do.			do.
	Z.3		do.	28.12.42	8. 8.43	do.
	Z.5		do.	20.12.42		do.
	Z.8		do.			do.
	Z.9		do.			do.
	Z.12		do.			do.
	Z.13	Townsville	do.	26. 1.43	21. 4.45	do.
	Z.14	Reception Camp, Q.	do.	17.11.43	22. 9.44	do. 2 AUST CORPS
	Z.15		do.			
	Z.16		do.			
	Z.17		do.			
	Z.18		do.			
AUST BASE P.O.	No.1	Cairo	North Africa	4. 7.41	31. 9.41	
	No.1	Tel el Kebir, Egypt	do.	2.10.41	26.12.42	
	2	Cairo	do.	4. 7.41	2.10.41	
	2	Adelaide	Pacific	–. 4.42		On mail from transport
	3	Cairo	North Africa	–. 7.41		
	4	do.	do.	4. 7.41		
	4	Tel el Kebir	do.	30.10.41	5. 5.42	
	17	Seremban	Malaya	31. 3.41	3. 1.42	
	18	Port Dickson	do.	7. 2.41	8. 2.42	
	19	Singapore	do.	27. 8.41	2.10.41	
	20	Mauccas	do.	1. 9.41	2.12.41	
	25		Malaya			)Doubtful if used
	26	Johore	do.	5.11.41	13. 2.42	)Sent to Malaya
	27		do.	16. 1.42	8. 2.42	)and lost there.
	28	Johore	do.	30.11.41	15. 1.42	
BASE P.O.	B.W.1.	Jerusalem	Palestine	26. 2.40	7. 7.40	BASE H.Q., A.I.F.
	B.W.1.	Gaza	do.	6. 8.40	2. 1.42	
BASE P.O. 1.M.D.	01	Brisbane	Pacific			
	02	do.	do.	14. 4.42	–. –.44	
BASE P.O. 2.M.D.	03	Sydney	do.	14.10.42	2. 7.43	

ARMY

Postmark	No.	Place	Campaign	Earliest Date	Latest Date	Remarks
BASE P.O. 2.M.D.	04	Sydney	Pacific	29. 3.42	28.10.42	
	05	do.	do.	21.11.42		
	06	do.	do.	23.11.42		
BASE P.O. 3.M.D.	07	Melbourne	do.	−. 5.43		
	08	do.	do.			
	09	do.	do.			
	010	do.	do.			
BASE P.O. 4.M.D.	011	Adelaide	do.			
	012	do.	do.	18. 5.42	22. 5.42	
	012	Papua	do.	15.12.42		
BASE P.O. 5.M.D.	013	Perth, W.A.	do.			
	014	do.	do.	11. 3.42	19. 6.43	
BASE P.O. 6.M.D.	015	Hobart, Tas.	do.	8. 9.45		
	016	do.	do.			
BASE P.O. 7.M.D.	017	Adelaide River, N.T.	do.	22. 7.41	13. 4.42	MIL P.O.1.
	018	do.	do.	31. 7.41	9. 4.42	MIL P.O.1.
BASE POST OFFICE	No.5	Queensland	Pacific	27. 9.39		
No. 1 ADV. BASE P.O.	1	Brisbane	Pacific	3.11.42	23. 7.43	
	2	do.	do.	4. 5.43		
No. 2 ADV. BASE P.O.	4	Adelaide	do.			
	6	do.	do.	18.11.42		
No. 3 AUST ADV. BASE P.O.	A	Townsville	do.	−. −.43	22. 5.45	
	B	do.	do.	2.12.43		
No. 4 AUST ADV. BASE P.O.	A		do.			
	B		do.			
	C		do.			

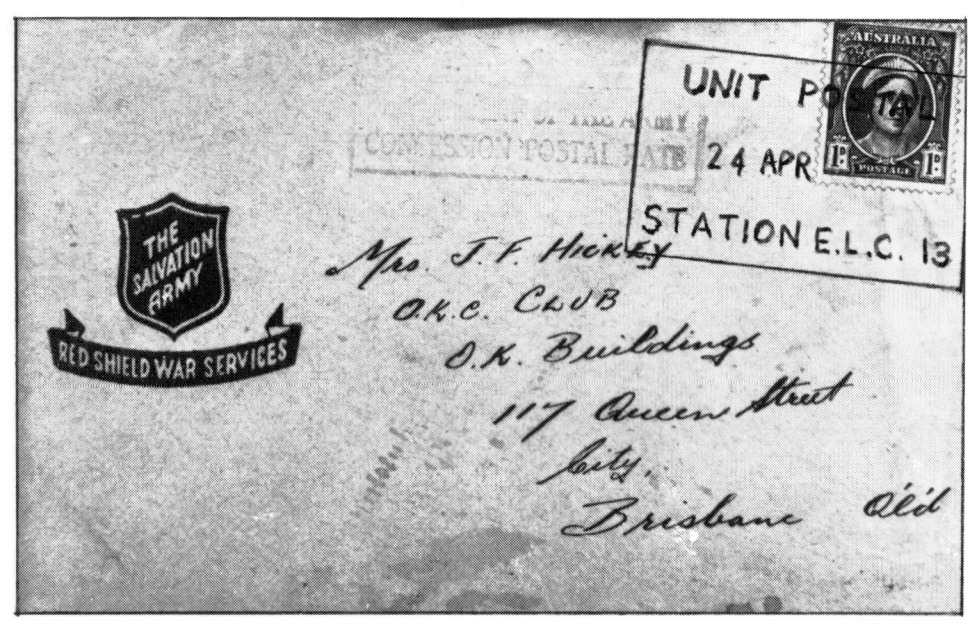

Unit Postal Station E.L.C. 13 – Pacific

2nd Bde. Hq. P.O. W.2 – Khassa, Palestine

ARMY

Postmark	No.	Place	Campaign	Earliest Date	Latest Date	Remarks
No. 7 AUST ADV. BASE P.O.		)First @ Lae,				
	A	)then Madang	Pacific	23. 8.44	7. 4.45	
	B	)and later @	do.	8. 4.45		
	C	)Torokina	do.	7. 8.44	18.11.45	
	D	Buna	do.	20. 8.44		
No. 1 AUST BASE P.O.	A	Sydney	Pacific	30. 7.43		
	C	do.	do.	28. 7.43	13.11.45	
	D	do.	do.	6. 8.43	6. 4.45	
	E	do.	do.	28. 8.43		
	F	do.	do.	15. 9.43		
No. 2 AUST BASE P.O.	A	Melbourne	do			
	B	do.	do.	26. 2.44	24. 9.45	
	C	do.	do.	7. 8.44	8.12.44	
	D	do.	do.			
	E	do.	do.			
	F	do.	do.			
No. 3 AUST BASE P.O.	A	Brisbane	do.			
	B	do.	do.	18.11.43	11. 5.45	
	C	do.	do.			
	D	do.	do.			
	E	do.	do.	28.10.43		
	F	do.	do.	8.10.43	1.12.43	
No. 4 AUST BASE P.O.	A	Perth	do.			
	B	do.	do.	18. 1.43		
	C	do.	do.	22. 8.43		
	D	do.	do.			
	E	do.	do.			
	F	do.	do.			
No. 5 AUST BASE P.O.	A	Adelaide	do.			
	B	do.	do.			
	C	do.	do.			
	D	do.	do.			
	E	do.	do.			
	F	do.	do.			
No. 6 AUST BASE P.O.	A	Borneo	do.	26. 7.45	1.12.45	
	B	do.	do.	10. 8.45	20.11.45	
	C	do.	do.	27.12.45	26.11.45	

ARMY

Postmark	No.	Place	Campaign	Earliest Date	Latest Date	Remarks
No. 6 AUST BASE P.O.	D	do. Kuching	Pacific	15. 9.45		
	E	do. Moratai	do.	31. 5.45	2. 8.45	
	F	do. Moratai	do.	1. 9.45		
No. 7 AUST BASE P.O.	A)		do.	20. 7.44	21.11.45	
	B)	First @ Port	do.	16.10.44	12. 6.45	
	C)	Moresby but	do.	9. 9.44	18. 4.45	
	D)	later @ Lae	do.	23.11.44		
	E)	or Torokina	do.	20. 6.44	4. 4.45	
	F)		do.	4.12.44	7. 1.45	
No. 8 AUST BASE P.O.	A	Kure	Japan	1.12.47	28.10.51	
	B	do.	do.	3. 6.46		
	C)	do.	do.	17. 5.46	14. 5.49	
	C)		Korea	27.12.50	8.12.53	
	D		Japan	25. 3.55		
1st BGE H.Q.P.O.	M.1)	Qastira	Palestine	23. 2.40	17. 4.40	
	M.1)	Egypt	North Africa	11. 9.40	4. 3.41	6 DIV. 16 BDE.
	M.1)		Greece	4. 4.41	24. 4.41	
	P.1	Kido. 89	Palestine	22.12.40	17. 2.43	
	W.1	Mughazi	do.	4.12.40	25. 9.42	
2nd BDE H.Q.P.O.	M.2)	Egypt	North Africa	7.10.40	24. 3.41	17 BDE. 6 DIV.
	M.2)		Greece	−. 3.41	24. 4.41	
	P.2	Sollum, then Tobruk	North Africa	9. 1.41	8.10.41	
	W.2)	Khassa	Palestine	20.12.40	9. 7.41	
	W.2)	Qastira Camp	Palestine	−.10.41	16. 1.42	
3rd BDE H.Q.P.O.	M.3)		do.	30.12.40	4.10.41	
	M.3)	Port Moresby	Pacific	−. 3.42	11. 6.42	
	P.3	Kilo 89	Syria	10.10.40	21.10.41	25 BDE
	W.3)	Egypt	North Africa	29.11.40	19. 3.41	
	W.3)		Greece		24. 4.41	
	W.3)		Crete	29. 4.41	9. 5.41	
DIV. H.Q.P.O.	D.M.1)	Cairo	North Africa	17.10.40	24. 2.41	
	D.M.1)	Piraeus	Greece	3. 4.41	24. 4.41	
	D.W.1	Barbara Hill 95	Palestine	13.10.40	−. 2.42	
DIV. SUPPLY H.Q.P.O.	S.M.1	Julio	Palestine	27. 2.40	4.10.40	
	S.P.1)	Barbara	do.	−. 5.40	−. 9.40	
	S.P.1)	Egypt	North Africa	3. 1.41	18. 3.41	

ARMY

Postmark	No.	Place	Campaign	Earliest Date	Latest Date	Remarks
DIV. SUPPLY H.Q.P.O.	S.P.1)		Greece		24. 4.41	
	S.W.1)	Egypt	North Africa	–. 4.41		
	S.W.1)		Greece	5. 3.41	8. 3.41	
ARMY SIGNALS –			North Africa	15. 5.42	11.11.43	
RAILHEAD P.O.	R.M.1)	Gaza Ridge	Palestine	1. 3.40	16. 4.40	2/1 AGH
	R.M.1)	T.P.O.	Palestine	–. 5.40	19. 3.41	
	R.M.1)		Greece	–. 4.41		
	R.W.1)	Deir Seneia	Palestine	–. 5.41	17. 2.42	
	R.W.1)	Rehovat	do.	1. 1.43		

AIR FORCE

Postmark	No.	Place	Campaign	Earliest Date	Latest Date	Postal Unit	Remarks
A.F.P.O. R.A.A.F. JAPAN	28	Bofu	Japan	–. –.46	20. 7.47	8	
	No.30)	Iwakuni	do.	–. –.46	15.12.53		
	No.30)		Korea	28. 7.54	6.12.55		
A.F.P.O.	25	Daly Waters N.T.	Pacific			8	
	No.25	57 Mile N.T.	do.	10. 9.42	30. 8.45		
	26	Gorrie N.T.	do.		17. 5.45	8	
	No.26	do. N.T.	do.	4. 5.43	7. 4.45	8	
	27	Horne Island, Torres Strait	do.			6	
	No.27	Sauler N.T.	do.	16. 1.43	21. 9.44	8	
	No.71	Townsville, Q.	do.	23.10.43		6	
	No.72	Cairns, Q.	do.	29. 6.43	3. 9.45	6	
	No.73)	Horne Island, Torres Strait	do.	14.10.43	28. 2.44	6	)These two)handstamps)differ)slightly
	No.73)	Tarakan, Borneo	do.	2. 5.45	8.12.45	11	
	No.74	Port Moresby, Papua	do.	11. 3.43	25. 5.45	7	In purple "A.F.P.O." across
	No.200)	Wards Field, Moresby	do.	2.12.42	5. 4.44	7	
	No.200)	Jackson's Field, Moresby	do.	6. 7.44	1. 6.45		
	No.201	Milne Bay, Papua	do.	2.11.42	18. 2.46	7	
	202)	Nadzab, A.N.G.	do.	2. 8.43		7	

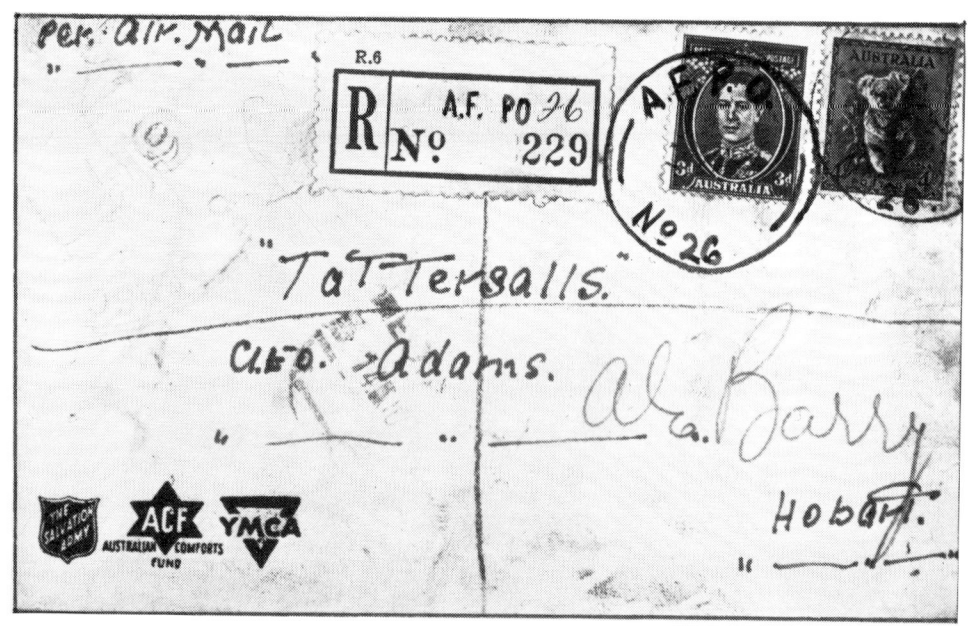

A.F.P.O. No. 26 – Gorrie, N.T.

A.F.P.O. No. 73 – Horne Island, Torres Strait

AIR FORCE

Postmark	No.	Place	Campaign	Earliest Date	Latest Date	Postal Unit	Remarks
A.F.P.O.	202	Lae, A.N.G.	Pacific	20. 1.45	25. 5.46		
	203)	Berry, Papua	do.	5. 2.43	2.10.43	7	
	203)	Manus, Admiralty Island	do.	28. 2.44	28.10.45		
AIR FORCE P.O.	No.20	Daly Waters N.T.	Pacific	3. 9.42	2. 5.45	8	
	20	Katherine N.T.	do.			8	
	No.21	Darwin, N.T.	do.	28. 6.43	5. 3.45	8	
	21	do.	do.	−. 1.43	14. 9.45	8	
	No.22	Batchelor, N.T.	do.	3. 8.42	1. 8.45	8	
	22	do.	do.			8	
	No.23	Katherine, N.T.	do.	17.10.42	3. 8.45	8	
	23	Melville Bay N.T.	do.	17. 5.44		8	
	No.24	Berdum, N.T.	do.	5.11.42	23. 2.45	8	
	No.25	Daly Waters N.T.	do.	19. 1.44		8	
	28	Fenton, N.T.	do.	17. 7.44	7. 6.45	6	
	31	Frognal, Vic.	do.				
	30	Iwakuri	Korea				
	50	Exmouth Gulf, W.A.	Pacific	18. 6.43	10.11.45	9	
	51	Onslow, W.A.	do.	16. 6.43	16.10.43	9	
	52	Corunna Downs, W.A.	do.	4.11.43	28. 5.45	9	
	53	Australia	do.				
	54)	Tacloban, Leyte Is.	do.			11	
	54)	San Miguel, Luzon Is.	do.	27. 4.45	22.10.45		
	56	Labuan	do.	−.10.45			Used to assist 234
	No.71	Townsville, Q.	do.	29. 9.42	18. 1.46	6	Has "QLD AUST" in mark.
	No.73	Tarakan, Borneo	do.	2. 5.45	18.12.45	11	
	No.74	Port Moresby	do.	20. 8.43	−. 3.46	7	
	76	Iron Range, Q.	do.	26. 5.43	1. 7.44	6	
	77	Cooktown, Q.	do.	14. 7.44	30. 9.44	6	
	78)	Karumba, Q.	do.	11. 6.43	25. 9.43	6	
	78)	Higginsfield, Cape York	do.	28. 6.43	13. 3.45	6	

45

AIR FORCE

Postmark	No.	Place	Campaign	Earliest Date	Latest Date	Postal Unit	Remarks
AIR FORCE P.O.	79	Middleburg, Nr. Biak Is. D.N.G.	Pacific	23. 4.45	26. 9.45	7	
	80)	Coonac, Vic.	do.	1. 5.44	31. 1.45		W.A.A.A.F. CAMP
	) 80)	Hollandia, D.N.G.	do.	1. 2.45	9. 2.46	7	
	No.201	Milne Bay, Papua	do.	12.11.42	16. 2.46	7	
	No.202	Lae	do.	18. 5.45	25. 5.46	7	
	No.207		do.				
	226		do.			7	
	233	Goodenough Is. Papua	do.	11. 6.43	20. 1.45		
	No.233	Jacquinot Bay, New Guinea	do.	6. 9.44	13. 9.45	11	
	234)	Noemloor, D.N.G.	do.	21. 7.44	27. 4.45	11	
	234)	Labuan	do.	12. 6.45	2. 4.46	11	Head Office of 11
	236	Finschhafen, New Guinea	do.	3. 6.43	−. 7.46	7	
	No.236	do. do.	do.			7	
	238	Madang, New Guinea	do.	11. 9.43	2. 4.46	7	
	250	Merauke, D.N.G.	do.			6	
	No.250	do.	do.	29. 9.42	18. 1.46	6	
	252		do.	20. 6.44	22.10.45	7	
	253		do.			7	
	254	Balikpapan, Borneo	do.	6. 9.44	28. 9.44	11	
AIR FORCE POST OFFICE	No.53	Noonkanbar, W.A.	Pacific	3.11.43	10. 3.45	9	
	No.34	Manila	do.	26. 8.45			
	No.238	Madang, New Guinea	do.	11. 9.43	2. 4.46	7	
	No.251	Morotai, East Indies	Pacific	1.11.44	−. −.49	11	
	No.252	Aitape, New Guinea	do.	10. 5.44	23. 2.46	7	
	No.253)	Cape Gloucester, New Guinea	do.	15. 3.44	23. 6.44	7	
	No.253)	Biak, D.N.G.	do.	15. 1.45	11. 2.46	7	

AIR FORCE

Postmark	No.	Place	Campaign	Earliest Date	Latest Date	Postal Unit	Remarks
AIR FORCE POST OFFICE							
	No.254)	San Jose, Mindoro	Pacific	25. 8.44	18. 6.45	11	
	No.254)	Balikpapan	do.	3. 7.45	9. 1.46	11	
R.A.A.F. AUSTRALIA							
	4100	Canberra, A.C.T.	Pacific	18.11.40			
	4101	Denelequin	N.S.W.	25. 8.41	31. 5.46		
	4102	Evans Head	do.	21.10.40	30. 6.48		
	4103	Lindfield	do.	1. 8.40	12.12.47		
	4104	Narrandera	do.	6.12.40	19. 2.45		
	4105	Narromine	do.	20.11.40	31. 8.46		
	4106	Nowra	do.	8. 5.42	18. 3.46		
	4107	Parkes	do.	23. 9.40	4.11.44		
	4108	Rathmines	do.	2.10.40	31.12.46		
	4109	Richmond	do.	1. 3.39	2. 3.45		
	4110	Temora	do.	14. 7.41	24.10.45		
	4111	Toarmwal	do.	7.12.42	30. 9.46		
	4112	Uranquinty	do.	16.12.41	14. 9.46		
	4113)	Wagga Wagga	do.	24. 7.40	1. 8.44		
	4113)	Allonville	do.	1. 8.44	1. 8.53		
	4114	Williamtown	do.	21. 7.41	26. 2.45		
	4115	Banktown	do.	2. 8.43	11. 9.53		
	4116	Dubbo	do.	1. 7.44	31. 8.46		
	4117	3 S.T.T. Ultimo	do.	20. 3.44	20. 7.45		
	5200	Ascot Vale	Victoria	16. 6.40	30. 3.46		
	5201	Laverton	do.	1. 6.38	25.11.40		Two Types
	5202	Point Cook	do.	4. 3.41	11.12.43		
	5203	West Melbourne	do.	16.11.42	28. 9.45		
	5204	Exhibition	do.	26. 3.41	4.10.46		
	5205	Nhill	do.	22. 9.41	31. 1.46		
	5206	Rocklands Dam	do.	27. 8.42	24.10.44		
	5207	Lake Boga	do.	14. 1.43	30. 4.46		
	5208	Shepperton	do.	23. 2.42	23. 6.45		
	5209	Benalla	do.	27. 6.41	26.10.46		
	5210	Ballarat	do.	25.11.40	19.10.46		
	5211	Somers	do.	11. 9.40	30. 6.46		
	5212	Cressy	do.	10. 3.43	27. 4.43		
	5213	Mildura	do.	17. 8.42	31. 5.46		
	5214	Bairnsdale	do.	20. 5.43	9. 3.46		
	5215	Sale	do.	12. 2.42	12. 1.46		
	5216	Sale East	do.	13. 4.43			

AIR FORCE

Postmark	No.	Place	Campaign	Earliest Date	Latest Date	Remarks
R.A.A.F.						
AUSTRALIA						
	5217	Frognal	Victoria	7. 6.43	30. 8.46	
	5218	Ransford	do.	26. 4.44	27.10.45	
	5219	Sandridge	do.	9.12.43	31. 8.47	
	6300	Amberley	Queensland	25.11.40	17.11.53	
	6301	Garbutt	do.	−. −.42	5. 9.49	
	6302	Sandgate	do.	18. 4.41	30. 9.46	
	6303	Bundaberg	do.	20.10.41	31. 7.46	
	6304	Maryborough	do.	8.12.41	31.12.45	
	6305	Kingaray	do.	7. 8.42	28. 2.46	
	6306	Loward	do.	26.10.42	28. 2.46	
	6307	Aitkenville	do.	22. 3.43	7. 1.46	
	6308	Drayton	do.	1. 7.43		
	6309	Breddan	do.	7. 9.43	30. 6.46	
	6310	Archerfield	do.	1.12.39	24. 2.48	
	6311	Oakey	do.	6. 3.44	17. 5.46	
	6312	Macrossan	do.	14. 9.44	15. 4.47	
	6313	Victoria Park	do.	21. 2.45	29. 6.46	
	7400	Mallala	South Australia	23.10.41	23. 5.46	
	7401	Mt. Gambier	do.	3. 3.41	5. 2.46	
	7402	4 S.T.T. Adelaide	do.	10. 2.43	29. 9.45	
	7403	Parafield	do.	20. 6.41	14. 5.46	
	7404	Port Pirie	do.	14. 7.41	1. 6.46	
	7405	Victor Harbor	do.	16. 2.42	14.10.45	
	7406)	Mitcham	do.	1. 7.43	10. 1.44	
	7406)	Springbank	do.	11. 1.44	28. 9.46	
	8500	Pearce	Western Australia	3. 3.42	28.11.45	
	8501	Cunderdin	do.	7. 1.41	31. 5.46	
	8502	Geraldton	do.	28. 4.41	31. 1.46	
	8503	Bussellton	do.	11. 7.42	31.10.45	
	8504	Clontarf	do.	20. 4.42	22.12.44	
	8505	Boulder	do.	8. 9.43	16. 3.46	
	8506	Yonchafr	do.	13. 3.44	6. 2.46	
	9600	Western Junction	Tasmania	10. 4.40	1. 6.45	

AIR FORCE

Postmark	No.	Place	Campaign	Earliest Date	Latest Date	Remarks
R.A.A.F. P.O. UNIT	No.5	Perth, W.A.	Pacific			
	No.6	Port Moresby, Papua	do.	29. 4.42	12.11.42	
	No.7	Darwin, N.T.	do.	13. 2.42	1. 7.46	
R.A.A.F. BASE P.O.	No.1	Melbourne	Pacific	10. 3.42	17.12.42	
	No.2	Sydney	do.	15. 5.43	19. 1.46	
	No.4	England	do.	−. 7.41	19. 2.42	Usually on re-directed mail.
	No.4	do.		1. 1.43	31. 7.43	English Type Double Circle.
	No.4	do.		7. 6.42	−. −.45	English Slogan Type.
	No.5	Cairo	Africa	27. 6.42	19. 2.46	
	No.11	Morotai, Dutch East Indies	Pacific	1.11.44	31.12.48	
	No.6	Port Moresby	do.			
	No.7	Darwin	do.			
R.A.A.F. BASE P.O.	Perth	Perth	Pacific	6. 6.43	27.12.45	No Number
	London	England	−	10. 9.42	20. 1.43	No Number
	Adelaide	Adelaide	Pacific			No Number
	Brisbane	Brisbane	do.	20. 5.43	20. 1.46	No Number
	Melbourne	Melbourne	do.	−. 9.41	31.12.45	No Number
	Sydney	Sydney	do.	4.10.45		No Number
	Ceylon	Ceylon (?)	do.			

NAVY

Postmark	No.	Place	Campaign	Earliest Date	Latest Date	Remarks
R.A.N. POST OFFICE NUMBER	2	Madang, New Guinea	Pacific	−. −.44	−. 2.46	
	2	Dreger Harbour Finschhafen	do.	27. 2.46	20. 5.50	
	3	Manus Island	do.	−. 3.49	3. 5.50	
	4)	Biak Island	do.	23. 4.45	13. 5.45	
	4)	Morotai, East Indies	do.	18. 5.45	8. 4.46	
R.A.N.P.O. FINSCHHAFEN	No.2))	Finschhafen	Pacific			Rectangular Frame

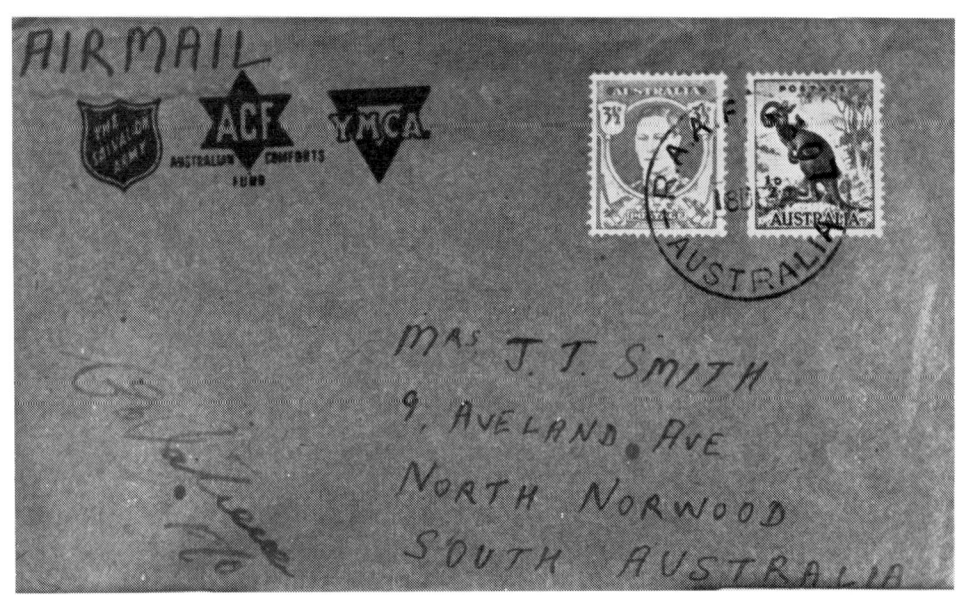

R.A.A.F. 6307 Australia – Aitkenville, Qld.

Mil. P.O. Mt. Martha, No. 1, Vic; Australia.

NAVY

Postmark	No.	Place	Campaign	Earliest Date	Latest Date	Remarks
NAVY POST OFFICE	No.1	Darwin	Pacific	−. 8.43	8.11.45	Circle
NAVY P.O.	No.1	Darwin	Pacific	−. 8.43	−. 9.43	Straight Line
NAVY P.O. DARWIN N.T.		Darwin	Pacific	−. 9.42	−. 4.43	Straight Line
H.M. TRANSPORT −		Used on H.M. Transports "Queen Mary" and "Queen Elizabeth"		−. −.42		Straight Line No Number; Two Sizes.
H.M. TRANSPORT −						Circle
H.M. TRANSPORT				2. 9.41	−.11.41	
	No.2			−. 1.40		Circle
	No.2					Straight Line
	No.4					do.
	No.5					do.
	No.5					Circle
	No.8					do.
	No.14					do.
	No.16			27. 4.44		do.
H.M.A.T.	Z			−. 9.40		Transport "Zealandia"

MILITARY POST OFFICES

Postmark	Place	Campaign	Earliest Date	Latest Date	Remarks
MIL. P.O.	Albury	New South Wales	20. 7.40		
	Bathurst	do.	28. 8.40	−. 7.46	
	Cowra	do.	4. 9.40	−. 3.46	
	Dubbo	do.	25. 9.40	−. 5.44	
	Glenfield	do.	30. 3.40	−. 3.45	
	Glen Lines No. 1	do.	−. 5.43	−. 6.43	
	Goulburn	do.	−. 1.46	−. 3.46	17 INF TNG BTN
	Greta	do.	6. 2.40	16. 3.47	
	Hay	do.	5.12.40	−. 8.46	
	Holdsworthy	do.	9. 5.41	7.10.43	
	Hume	do.	−.10.42	−. 9.45	Relief P/M "DG" (11.9.42)
	Ingleburn	do.	6.11.39	26. 3.46	
	Kenmore	do.	−. 3.45	−. 1.46	Changed to "Goulburn"
	Liverpool	do.	19.10.39	23. 6.50	
	Narellan	do.	6. 2.41	3. 7.46	
	Narromine	do.	−.12.40		
	Rutherford	do.	17.11.39	3.11.45	
	Showgrounds, Sydney	do.	22. 6.40	26. 9.46	

MILITARY POST OFFICES

Postmark	Place	Campaign	Earliest Date	Latest Date	Remarks
MIL. P.O.	Singleton	New South Wales	12. 2.42	−. 2.46	
	Tamworth	do.	19. 7.40	1. 1.44	No Number
	Tamworth No.1	do.	2. 3.42		
	Tamworth No.2	do.	3. 9.40	−. 9.45	
	Tenterfield	do.	−. 3.43	−. 1.45	
	Wagga Wagga	do.	29. 8.40 Reopened −.10.42	−. 3.47	
	Wallgrove	do.	18. 3.40	−.11.46	
	Warwick Farm	do.	28.12.40	−.11.42	
	Bribie Island	Queensland	26. 3.42	−. 9.44	
	Camp Cable	do.	−. 3.45	−. 2.46	
	Cabarlah	do.	16. 7.41	−. 4.46	
	Calounda	do.	−.12.39	−. 1.40	
	do. No.2	do.	27. 3.40	−. 3.41	
	Canungra	do.	−. 2.43	−. 6.46	
	Chermside	do.	−.11.40	−. 6.46	
	Cowan Cowan	do.	−.11.39	−.11.44	
	Grovelly	do.	11. 7.40	1. 8.45	
	Enaggera	do.	−.12.39	8. 6.47	
	Kalenga Park	do.	−.10.43	−. 9.45	
	Lytton	do.	28. 3.40	−.11.44	
	Milmerran	do.			
	Miowera	do.	4. 4.40	−. 2.41	
	Morgan Park	do.	2. 8.43	−. 1.45	
	Ravenshoe	do.	−. 9.43		
	Redbank	do.	2. 9.40	−.11.46	Relief P/M "P.M.G. Dept." (2.9.40)
	Rocky Creek	do.	−. 8.43	−.11.40	
	Sellheim	do.	−. 6.41	−. 1.45	
	Stuart	do.			
	Wacol	do.	14.11.45	17.11.53	
	Wallangorra	do.	28.11.41	−. 4.46	
	Yeerongrilly	do.	12.10.43	−. 6.46	
	Yeppoon	do.	17. 6.40	−. 7.42	
	Vic. Barracks, Brisbane		−. 8.41		
	Balcombe	Victoria	22. 6.40	4. 2.47	
	Bandiana	do.	−.10.42	10.11.47	
	Bendigo	do.	22. 7.40		
	do. No.2	do.	20. 7.40	−.11.41	
	Bittern	do.			
	Bonegilla	do.	25.10.40	−. 3.47	
	Broadmeadows	do.	14. 3.39	23. 7.51	
	Camp Pell	do.	−. 2.43	7. 3.47	
	Caulfield	do.	19. 4.40	−. 3.44	
	Colac	do.	1.10.40	−.11.43	
	Darby No.1	do.	3. 6.42	−. 8.42	Changed to "Foster"

MILITARY POST OFFICES

Postmark	Place	Campaign	Earliest Date	Latest Date	Remarks
MIL. P.O.	Darby	Victoria	5.10.40	8. 3.43	
	Dhurringle	do.	6. 6.40	−.10.40	P.O.W. Camp. Changed to "Tatura"
	Fishermen's Bend	do.	−.12.41	20. 1.47	
	Foster No.1	do.	11. 8.42	−. 2.43	From "Darby No.1"
	Geelong No.1	do.	20. 7.40	9.10.41	
	Geelong Racecourse	do.	−. 2.41	−. 4.41	
	Gherang	do.	28. 2.42	−.11.42	
	Ivanhoe	do.	−. 2.43	−. 1.44	
	Lysterfield Hills	do.	12. 3.42	−. 7.42	
	Mongalore No.1	do.	13. 8.42	−.11.42	
	Marbyrnong	do.	24.11.41		
	Mornington	do.			
	Mt. Martha No.1	do.	2.11.39	−.11.42	
	Murchison	do.	5.11.41	−. 4.47	
	Myrtleford	do.	5. 5.42	−. 4.46	
	Ocean Grove	do.			
	Puckapanyal No.1	do.	14.11.39	16.10.43	
	do.	do.	3.12.41	−.12.46	Machine Cancellation
	Rawville	do.	−. 4.42	−.11.43	
	Royal Park	do.	29.10.42	30.10.51	
	do. No.2	do.	11. 7.40	25. 1.47	
	Seymour No.1	do.	31.10.39	−. 8.41	To No.2
	do. No.2	do.	27.11.39	22. 9.41	To No.3
	do. No.3	do.	4.12.39		
	do. No.4	do.	15. 1.40	19. 4.45	To No. 29
	do. No. 5	do.	20. 1.40		To No. 25A
	do. No.10	do.		−. 3.46	
	do. No.17	do.	29. 8.41	−. 5.47	
	do. No.25	do.	−. 5.42		
	do. No. 25A	do.	−. 8.41		From No.5
	do. No.29	do.	−. 8.41	−.11.43	From No.4
	do. No.30	do.	19. 9.41	−.11.43	
	do. −	do.	−. 9.44		
	Shepparton	do.	22. 7.40		
	Showgrounds, Melbourne	do.	28.10.39	29. 5.42	To Ascot Vale R.A.A.F. P.O.
	Tatura No.1	do.	25.10.40	−. 4.47)	
	do. No.2	do.	−.10.40	−.12.41)	P.O.W. Camp
	do. No.3	do.	−.11.40	12. 2.47)	
	do. No.4	do.	−.11.40	−.11.42)	
	Torquay	do.	26. 1.40	13. 4.40	
	Wangaratta	do.	22. 7.40		
	Watsonia	do.	−.11.42	−.10.46	
	Werribee	do.	26. 9.40	−. 2.42	
	Williamtown W.17	do.	20. 4.40	−.11.42	
	Adelaide River	Northern Territory	−.10.41	−. 5.42	7 MD FIELD POSTAL UNIT H.Q.
	Alice Springs	do.	21. 4.41	−. 3.46	

MILITARY POST OFFICES

Postmark	Place	Campaign	Earliest Date	Latest Date	Remarks
MIL. P.O.	Darwin No.1	Northern Territory	4. 9.40	21.12.46	
	do. No.2	do.	3. 1.41	−. 4.42	
	do. No.3	do.	−. 6.41	−. 4.42	RELIEF 14 (11.6.41)
	do. No.4	do.	−. 8.41	−. 4.42	
	do. No.5	do.	14.10.41	−. 4.42	
	Parap	do.	−. 6.46	−. 2.47	? In N.T. or S.A.
	Larrakeyah	do.	−. 4.41	7. 5.41	
	New Barrow Creek Tel.		−. 9.42	−. 2.43	
	Exhibition Building	South Australia	−.11.45	−.11.46	
	Hampstead	do.	−.11.45	−. 8.46	
	Northfield	do.	−. 5.43	29. 5.46	
	Sandy Creek	do.	−.11.42	−. 9.43	
	Springbank	do.	21. 8.42	10. 3.47	
	Warradale	do.	21. 9.40	9. 8.43	
	Wayville	do.	−. 8.40	−.12.46	
	Woodside	do.	23. 1.40	−. 7.44	
	Woodside Military Camp		−. 2.40	−.11.42	
	Brighton	Tasmania	−.11.39	−.10.46	
	Launceston	do.	19. 2.40	−. 7.43	
	Mona Vale	do.	24. 9.40	−. 7.43	
	Belmont Park	Western Australia	27. 6.40	6. 6.41	
	Bunbury	do.	6. 1.41	30. 4.41	RELIEF "J" used 11.3.41
	Canning Weir	do.	14.10.40	23.12.40	
	Fort Swanbourne	do.	22. 1.40	−. 8.40	To Swanbourne Mil. P.O.
	Karrakatta	do.	1. 4.41	8. 7.44	
	Melville	do.	1. 1.40	30. 6.46	
	Naval Base	do.	28. 1.40 / −. 4.42	−. 8.40) / −.11.42)	Closed and then reopened
	Northam	do.	4.12.39	10. 4.43	
	Nungarin	do.	5. 1.44	15. 1.47	
	Showgrounds	do.	26. 3.40	16.12.44	RELIEF "1" used 8.7.40.
	Swanbourne	do.	17. 8.40	6. 8.51	From Fort Swanbourne
	Hollywood	do.	4.10.44	3. 3.47	

W.A.A.A.F. POST OFFICES

W.A.A.A.F. P.O.					
	Coonac	Victoria	−. 5.44		
	Larundel	do.	15. 3.43	−. 2.46	
	West Melbourne	do.	−. 1.43		

MILITARY HOSPITALS

Postmark	Place	Campaign	Earliest Date	Latest Date	Remarks
MIL.					
HOSPITAL	Baulkham	New South			
	Hills	Wales	−.11.43	−. 3.46	
	Concord	do.	−.11.41	20. 8.46	Still Open
	Randwick	do.	14. 3.34	27.12.40	
	Hiedelberg	Victoria	−. 2.42	27. 4.47	
	Hollywood	Western Australia	4.10.44	21. 3.47	
BASE					
HOSPITAL	Brisbane	Queensland	−. 1.47	18.12.51	

REPATRIATION HOSPITALS

Postmark	Place	Campaign	Earliest Date	Latest Date	Remarks
REPAT. GENL.					
HOSP.	Caulfield	Victoria	11. 7.35	−. 8.40	
	Hiedelberg	do.		2. 5.53	
REPAT. HOSP.					
	Greenslopes	Queensland	1. 4.50	13. 9.51	Still Open
REP. HOSP.	Hollywood	Western Australia	3. 3.47	10. 5.50	Still Open
REPAT. GENL.					
HOSP.	Springbank	South Australia	−. 3.47		

R.A.A.F. POST OFFICES

Postmark	Place	Campaign	Earliest Date	Latest Date	Remarks
R.A.A.F.					
P.O.	Allonville	New South Wales	−. 9.44	19. 7.50	
	Bankstown	do.	−.11.43		
	Denelequin	do.	−.10.41	−. 7.46	
	Dubbo	do.	−. 9.44	−. 9.46	? N.S.W. or QLD.
	Evans Head	do.	21.10.40	−.11.46	
	Lindfield	do.	12. 8.40	17. 5.50	
	Narrandera	do.	23. 1.41	−. 6.46	
	Narromine	do.	27. 1.41	−. 9.46	
	Nowra	do.	−. 7.42	−. 5.46	
	Parkes	do.	−. 2.41	−. 7.46	
	Rathmires	do.	−. 9.40	30. 6.52	

MĪL. P.O. Showgrounds, Melb, Vic., Aust

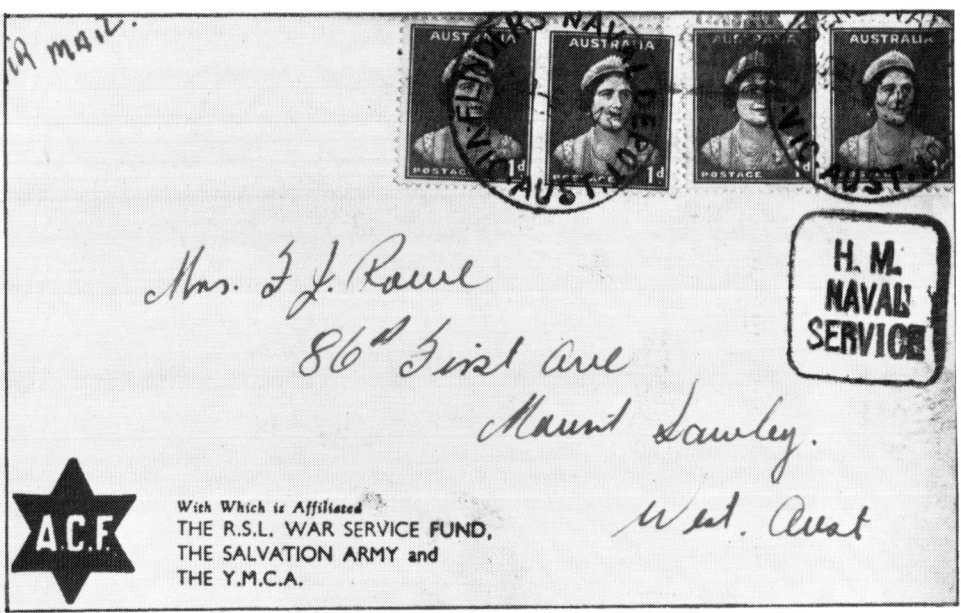

Flinders Naval Depot, Vic., Aust.

R.A.A.F. POST OFFICES

Postmark	Place	Campaign	Earliest Date	Latest Date	Remarks
R.A.A.F. P.O.	Richmond Aerodrome	N.S.W.	−. 7.39	−. 9.40	
	Richmond	do.	22. 8.40	14. 5.52	
	Schofields	do.	−. 9.46	9. 7.48	
	Tamworth	do.	24. 8.40	−. 9.49	
	Temora	do.	16. 8.41	−. 5.46	
	Tocumural	do.	23. 9.42	−.11.46	
	Ultimo	do.	−. 5.44	−. 9.45	
	Uranquinty	do.	−. 2.42	−.11.46	
	Wagga Wagga	do.	29. 8.40	−. 9.44	Changed to Allonville
	Williamtown	do.	2.10.41	19. 9.53	To 4114 ? Reopened 8.7.45
	Ascot Vale	Victoria	−. 2.42	−. 5.46	From Showgrounds Mil. P.O.
	Bairndale	do.	7.11.42	8. 9.53	
	Ballarat	do.	20. 9.40	−.10.46	
	Beralla	do.	−. 8.41	−.11.45	
	Cressy	do.	−. 5.43	−. 6.43	
	Exhibition No.3	do.	−. 4.41	−.11.46	
	Frognall	do.	−. 7.43	−.11.46	
	Laverton	do.	12.12.38	9.11.53	
	Lake Boga	do.	−. 2.43	−. 4.46	
	Mildura	do.	−. 9.42	−. 7.46	
	Nhill	do.	−.10.41	−. 3.46	
	Point Cook	do.	7. 2.42	22. 4.53	
	Ransford	do.	−. 5.44	−.11.45	
	Rocklands Dam	do.	−.10.42	−.11.44	
	Sale	do.	−. 3.42	−. 3.46	
	Sale East	do.	6.10.40	16. 6.52	
	Sandridge	do.	−. 1.44	26. 2.47	
	Shepparton	do.	−. 4.42	−. 9.45	
	Somers	do.	24.10.40	−.10.46	
	Tottenham	do.	20. 8.48	11. 6.53	
	Canberra	A.C.T.	−.11.40	10.11.46	

AIR FORCE POST OFFICES

Postmark	Place	Campaign	Earliest Date	Latest Date	Remarks
R.A.A.F. P.O.	Aitkenvale	Queensland	−. 5.43	−. 2.46	
	Amberley	do.	−. 1.41	23. 3.43	
	Archerfield Aerodrome	do.	−. 1.40	27. 5.43	
	Breddan	do.	−.11.43	−. 7.46	

AIR FORCE POST OFFICES

Postmark	Place	Campaign	Earliest Date	Latest Date	Remarks
R.A.A.F. P.O.	Bundaberg	Queensland	–.12.41	–. 9.46	
	Drayton	do.	–. 8.43		
	Garbutt	do.	–. 1.43		From Townsville
	Kingaroy	do.	–.10.42	–. 4.46	
	Lowood	do.	5.10.43	–. 4.46	
	Macrossan	do.	–.11.44	–. 5.47	
	Maryborough	do.	24.12.41	–. 2.46	
	Oakey	do.		–. 7.46	
	Sandgate	do.	30. 4.41	–.11.46	
	Townsville	do.	3. 2.41	–. 1.43	To Garbutt
	Victoria Park	do.			
	No.4 S.T.T. Adelaide	South Australia	–. 5.43	–.11.45	
	Mallala	do.	29.12.41	14. 7.46	
	Mitcham	do.	–. 8.43	–. 1.44	To Springbank
	Mouth Gambier	do.	19. 8.41	–. 3.46	
	Parafield	do.	–. 9.41	–. 7.46	
	Port Pirie	do.	28. 7.41	–. 7.46	
	Springbank	do.	–. 1.44	–.11.46	From Mitcham
	Victor Harbor	do.	–. 1.42	7. 9.43	
	Bussellton	Western Australia	24. 9.42	–.11.45	
	Clontarf	do.	–. 7.42	–. 1.45	
	Cunderain	do.	–. 2.41	–. 9.46	
	Dunreath	do.	19. 9.45	25. 5.46	
	Geraldton	do.	28. 8.41	31. 1.46	
	Pearce	do.	23. 9.40	–. 3.53	
	Yonchep	do.	15. 3.44	6. 2.46	
	Darwin No.1	Northern Territory	19. 8.40 / –. 3.46	5. 4.42 / 5. 9.53	Closed and then re-opened
	Western Territory	Tasmania	5.11.40	5. 2.41	
	Cocos Island	South Indian Ocean	–. 8.51	19.11.53	Still open
	Morotai	Dutch East Indies	3. 6.47	11. 9.47	

NAVAL POST OFFICES

Postmark	Place	Campaign	Earliest Date	Latest Date	Remarks
NAVAL P.O.	Balmoral	New South Wales	–. 7.45	2. 6.53	British Naval Barracks, Sydney

NAVAL POST OFFICES

Postmark	Place	Campaign	Earliest Date	Latest Date	Remarks
NAVAL P.O.	Herne Bay	New South Wales	18. 2.46	−. 8.46	
	Nowra	do.	15. 8.49	25. 8.53	
	Sydney R.N. Barracks	do.	−. 7.45	−. 7.46	
R.N. AIR STN.	R.N. Air Stn. Schofields	do.	−. 7.45	28. 6.53	
NAVAL DEPOT	Flinders Naval Depot	Victoria	23. 9.40	17. 1.52	Still Open
NAVAL BASE		Western Australia	22. 3.53		

R.A.N. SHORE ESTABLISHMENTS

Postmark		Place	Campaign
H.M.A.S.	− Assault	Port Stoffens	New South Wales
do.	− Cerbeus	Flinders	Victoria
do.	− Huon	Hobart	Tasmania
do.	− Knuttabal	Sydney	New South Wales
do.	− Leenwin	Fremantle	Western Australia
do.	− Lonsdale	Melbourne	Victoria
do.	− Majestic	Townsville	Queensland
do.	− Maitland	Newcastle	New South Wales
do.	− Melville	Darwin	Northern Territory
do.	− Moreton	Brisbane	Queensland
do.	− Penguin	Sydney	New South Wales
do.	− do. II	do.	do.
do.	− Platypus	Cairns	Queensland
do.	− Rushcutter	Edgecliffe	New South Wales
do.	− Torrens	Adelaide	South Australia

P.O.W. CAMPS

N.S.Wales P.O.W. P.O.	Cowra	New South Wales	27.12.43

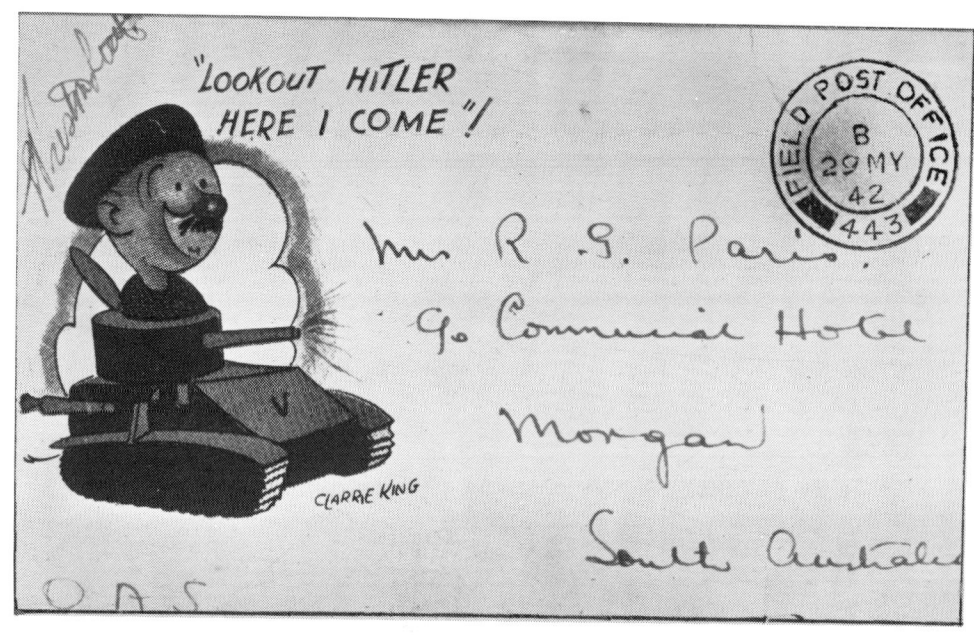

Field Post Office 443 – Alexandria, Egypt

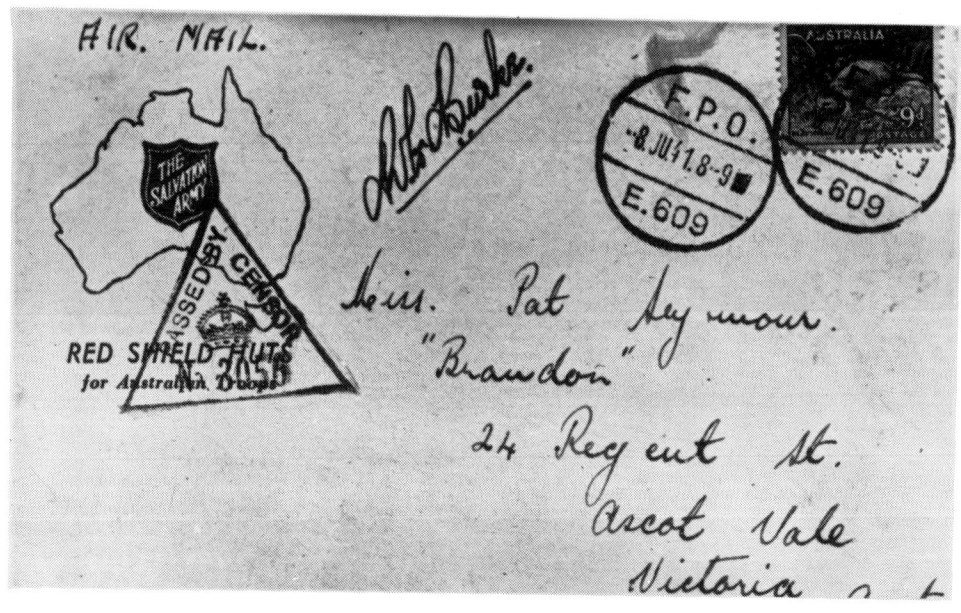

F.P.O. E. 609 – Hill 69, Palestine

ENGLISH TYPE
(FOUND USED ON AUSTRALIAN STAMPS OR USED BY AUSTRALIAN FORCES)

Postmark	No.	Place	Campaign	Earliest Date	Latest Date	Remarks
FIELD POST OFFICE	26		North Africa	−.11.40	−.11.44	
	28		do.	−.11.40	−.10.43	
	40		France	24. 4.40		
	121		Palestine			
	122)		Palestine			
	122)		Greece	7. 3.41		
	122)	Nikosia	Cyprus	10. 5.41	−. 8.41	
	123		do.			
	155	Tobruk	North Africa	−.10.41	17.12.41	13 BTN of 20 BDE
	170		Greece			
	171		Greece	2. 6.41		
	175		do.	−. 4.41	26. 4.41	6 AGH
	176		do.	−. 4.41		
	177		do.	−. 4.41		
	183		do.	−. 4.41		
	190		do.	−. 3.41	26. 3.41	
	192		do.	7. 4.41		
	193		do.	26. 3.41		
	194		do.	−. 4.41		
	195		do.	−. 4.41		
	245		North Africa	14. 3.41		
	221		Crete	−. 4.41	1. 6.41	6 DIV.
	353/7	(All)	Malaya		15. 2.42	18 DIV.
	443)	Salisbury Plain	Gt. Britain	6. 8.40		18 AUST. BDE
	443)	Alexandria	North Africa	7. 1.41	−.11.44	
	444)	Alton, Hants	Gt. Britain	29. 7.40	−. 8.40	AUST. RLY. CONtn. AUST. FOR. CO.
	444)	Ikringi Morgut	Palestine	−. 2.41	−. 4.44	
	445)	Salisbury Plain	Gt. Britain	6. 8.40		
	445)	Hill 95 & Rehovat	Palestine	1. 8.41	27. 1.42	
	450)	Woolmer, Hants.	Gt. Britain	11. 9.40	−. −.41	
	450)	H.M. Transport		−. 4.41	2. 6.41	Used on H.M. Transport only.
	552	Beirut	Syria	−. 7.42	−. 1.43	9 DIV RLY CONst.
	707		Korea			
	740		Korea	12. 7.52		
	790		Korea	6.11.51		
	798		Korea			B.A.P.O.3.
	847		Gt. Britain	−. 9.44	−. 9.44	Sept. 1944 only. A.I.F. attached to Home Depot.
	915			24. 3.43		

ENGLISH TYPE
(FOUND USED ON AUSTRALIAN STAMPS OR USED BY AUSTRALIAN FORCES)

Postmark	No.	Place	Campaign	Earliest Date	Latest Date	Remarks
FIELD POST OFFICE	946	Iwakui	Japan		−. −.55	B.A.P.O.5.
	948	Seoul	Korea	26. 2.55		B.A.P.O.3.
	949	Kure	Japan			B.A.P.O.5.
	949		Korea	22. 7.49	3. 7.53	
BRITISH FLEET MAIL	5	Fremantle	Western Australia	30. 5.46	−. 4.50	
	9	Adelaide	South Australia	−. −.44	23.12.49	In 1950 this mark was used in Hong Kong.
	12	Sydney	New South Wales	30. 5.45	−. −.49	
	16	Darwin	Northern Territory	−. −.44	−. −.49	
	25	Manus Island	Pacific	25.10.50		
	34	Brisbane	Queensland	18.12.45	−. −.49	
HOME DEPOT R.E.P.S.	7		Gt. Britain	−.11.40	−. 5.41	A.I.F. attached to Home Depot.
M.P.O.	E.601	Cairo	North Africa	−. 4.40	10. 8.40)	
B.P.O.	E.602	Alexandria	do.	−. 4.40	1. 9.40)	
M.P.O.	E.602 (	Army Audit (Office, Cairo	do.	−. 4.40	)	
	E.603	Suez	do.	27. 2.40	−.10.41)	
	E.604)	Egypt	do.	−. 4.40	)	
	E.604))	Agordat, Eritrea	do.	27. 3.44	)	
F.P.O.	E.605	Alexandria	do.	28. 2.41	30. 5.41)	
	E.606	Suez	do.	−. −.40	)	
M.P.O.	E.607)	Sidi Gaber	do.	14. 8.40	−. 7.41)	
	E.607)	Tel Aviv	Palestine	−.10.42	)	
	E.608)	Suez Canal	North Africa	−. 4.41	1.12.41)	
	E.608)	Atherton, Q.	Australia	−. 4.42	13. 9.42)	
F.P.O.	E.609	Hill 69	Palestine	−. 5.41	30. 7.41)	
	E.610	do.	do.	−. −.40	)	
	E.611	Julis	do.	−. 5.41	10. 7.41)	

F.P.O. = Field Post Office
M.P.O. = Military Post Office
B.P.O. = Base Post Office
This type of postmark is often found on Army "Seals."

EGYPTIAN TYPE
(FOUND USED ON AUSTRALIAN STAMPS OR USED BY AUSTRALIAN FORCES)

Postmark	No.	Place	Campaign	Earliest Date	Latest Date	Remarks
EGYPT POSTAGE PREPAID	5	Qassassin	North Africa	4. 9.41	4. 2.44	
	6		do.	4. 9.41		

EGYPTIAN TYPE
(FOUND USED ON AUSTRALIAN STAMPS OR USED BY AUSTRALIAN FORCES)

Postmark	No.	Place	Campaign	Earliest Date	Latest Date	Remarks
EGYPT POSTAGE PREPAID	7	Tel-el-Kebir	North Africa	4. 9.41	11.10.41	
	8	Cairo	do.	23. 3.41	22. 3.42	AUST. BASE
	16	El Ballah	do.			
	17	Heliopolis	do.	17.10.42		
	18		do.	11.10.41		
	21	El Ballah	do.	10. 7.42		
	22		do.			
	25		do.			
	26		do.			
	30		do.	24. 5.43		
	31	Cairo	do.			
	34		do.			
	37		do.			
	40	Almaza	do.	2.11.40	7.11.42	
	41	Ikingi Maryut	do.	17. 5.41	7. 6.41	
	42	Cairo	do.			N.Z.F.P.O.
	45	Moascar	do.			
	55		do.			H.Q.R.A.F.
	58	Cairo	do.	20. 6.41		
	61	Alexandria	do.	9. 5.41	23. 5.41	
	64		do.			
	66		do.	30.10.41		
	72		do.			
	80		do.			
	85		do.			
	93		do.			
	103		do.			
	137		do.			
	143		do.			
	152		do.			

INDIAN TYPE
(FOUND USED ON AUSTRALIAN STAMPS OR USED BY AUSTRALIAN FORCES)

Postmark	No.	Place	Campaign	Earliest Date	Latest Date	Remarks
F.P.O.	29	Kuala Lumpur	Malaya	−. 2.41	6. 3.41	
	32A	Selangor	do.	18.11.41	26. 1.42	
	50		do.			
	50A		do.			
	50B		do.			

NEW ZEALAND TYPE
(FOUND USED ON AUSTRALIAN STAMPS OR USED BY AUSTRALIAN FORCES)

Postmark	No.	Place	Campaign	Earliest Date	Latest Date	Remarks
M.P.O.	K.W.5		Syria	16. 3.42		

AMERICAN TYPE
(FOUND USED ON AUSTRALIAN STAMPS OR USED BY AUSTRALIAN FORCES)

Many covers are to be found coming within this category, but as one of our members is already working on such a list which will shortly be made available to our members, it has been decided to omit this section.

(Note to the Second edition)
Unfortunately, the list mentioned above (in original edition) has not matured, and the student is referred to "Locations and Assignments, U.S. Army Post Offices, World War II," compiled for the War Cover Club of America by A.J. Tripp, which lists most of the locations of the American type postmarks used on Australian stamps.

Rare Cover From Dutch soldier in Australian Hospital at Balikpapan

in Borneo Oilfields, Netherlands East Indies (Dutch Censor mark)